KISSING
DEAD
GIRLS

Daphne Gottlieb

SOFT SKULL PRESS
NEW YORK

Library of Congress Cataloging-in-Publication Data

Gottlieb, Daphne, 1968–
  Kissing dead girls / Daphne Gottlieb.
    p. cm.
  ISBN-13: 978-0-9796636-5-9 (alk. paper)
  ISBN-10: 0-9796636-5-2 (alk. paper)
  I. Title.

PS3557.O829K57 2008
811'.54—dc22

                                      2006100989

Book design by David Barnett
Printed in the United States of America

Soft Skull Press
New York, NY

www.softskull.com

table of contents

Thanks to: Soft Skull Press, especially Richard Nash, and the San Francisco Literation Front, without whom this book would likely not exist, and to Kirsten Saxton, Nick Mamatas, and Marty McConnell whose keen eyes were a huge help. Thanks to the Atlantic Center for the Arts, where this book was first completed in residency. With love and thanks too to Claudius Reich. With love to all the dead girls I've loved before (even those who are boys).

Grateful thanks to the following publications in which pieces from this book first appeared: *Bottoms Up, Bullets & Butterflies, Columbia Poetry Review, With a Rough Tongue: Femmes Write Porn, Five Fingers Review, failbetter.com, In the Criminal's Cabinet, Instant City, McSweeney's Internet Tendencies, MiPoesias, Red Light: Superheroes, Saints and Sluts* and *Washington Square*.

All genders and pronouns herein
are intended to reflect a range.

KISSING

DEAD

GIRLS

mouth-to-mouth

no one would believe it, that a kiss could bring you back to life: dead for so long, still for how long, but that kiss started you breathing again, because of her kiss your lungs ached for the first time in how long, filling with air where there'd only been dust; those lips touched yours and then yours were moving —moving—not in sleep or resistance but in pleasure and your mouth moved and her mouth moved and so much—it must be the kiss—what was your body before this? where were you before? your backbone a colony of electric eels, the stars now hidden inside your hands; your head swarmed with fireflies and all the world you've been missing: trees, economic upswings and downturns, wars, the dog's death last fall, stores in your neighborhood filled and emptied and all this information, last Christmas, tsunami, all this time, how many species extinct, that mouth, how many dead languages still caught between your teeth and now silent, speaking the future in tongues, this kiss, you are awake and it's been so long, the world is so loud, that tongue is licking the death out of your mouth, sucking the poison out of your bite, your body is screaming and you are nothing but kiss anymore just kiss just kiss and as those lips pull away from you, it's impossible to know if all this is because of the kiss or because of her, because of him, the kisser or the kiss, you are awake, you are just meat, you want to be cut up, packaged and sold and consumed, ground between molars, that nourishing and wrecked at once, and that mouth is pulling away, that mouth is pulling away and you see her face, you see his face looking at yours, your mouth is a monster, is making history, is making a word, your mouth is your arms pulling that body close to you again, forming the oh, the pucker, the nothing except *more*

how to make a dead girl

1 part declined body temperature

1 part inconvertible lactic acid at atmospheric temperature[*]

1 part lividity[†]

1 part decomposition[‡]

5 parts myth[§]

---

[*]   Which century is this? Where does this dead girl belong? How long has she been dead for? The temperature of the body tells a story. As she goes from warm and soft and pliable to warm and stiff, the dead-girl clock reads between three and eight hours. The story is primed, ready.

[†]   After the heart has given up beating, the blood ceases circulating throughout the body. Gravity pulls it down. Within a couple hours of death, the areas that the blood coagulates in turn blue or purple, like bruises.

You can call the heart, beating or otherwise, a wholly natural thing, sex. The solid blood? Also sex. The assassin who stopped her heart, the poison, the virus that demands she perform for us, that's gender. We're all performing right along with her. Even the killer. Her heart hasn't started again. She's blue because she can't move. It's time to get the blood moving again. Kiss the dead girl and she'll awaken. Dead girls have sex on their a/gender.

[‡]   Exposition: Parasites (protagonists) find the body (antagonist) quickly. Everyone wants a piece of the dead girl. Death becomes them.

Rising Action: The ants come marching one by one.

Climax: Her own body consumes her, feeding herself with itself until she breaks wide open to the world and the world comes rushing into her. No inside, no outside.

Falling Action: Her body broken open is no longer hers. She is now E. coli, ants, flies, vultures. She is something other than who she was when the denouement comes around. She has changed but we have been transformed, watching her. We have transformed her, watching.

[§]   She decides not to go to grandma's house after all. She just wants a few more pills since they're not working. She has been asleep for more than 100 years. She wants to go swimming. She hates apples, no thanks. She goes grocery shopping. She's not pregnant, thank god. She's in the woods with her brother and they're holding hands and it won't get dark for hours and they keep walking.

destroyer of all things[*]

Kali says, when I bring her a bottle of wine, *What? You think you can get me drunk and take advantage of me?* When I show up with fine Belgian chocolates, she accuses me of trying to kill her, since the chocolates have nuts. *And,* she sniffs, *it's such a small box.* I bring her daisies and she snorts that *it figures I don't think enough of her to bring roses.* When I bring her roses, she smiles. *How beautiful,* she says, *these will look on your grave.*

---

[*] "destroyer of all things" is modeled after Lydia Davis' "The Mother" from *Break it Down.*

pilot light

I've been wrecked by Amelia Earhart. When she's not around, I nuzzle the fuzz on the inside of her leather cap's earflaps, finger the soft folds of her tan aviator's jacket. When she nonchalantly breezes through the room, slings her jacket over her shoulder, matador-like, I thrill to the fact that my fingerprints, the tiniest morsels of my skin, travel with her.

She always knows exactly where she is. I only know by my proximity to her. To Amelia's left. To her right. 5,000 miles away. Beyond my grasp. Right now, she's doing something with a map and a compass at the table, sipping her coffee. Now she's calculating something on its edge. Now she's talking out loud, and I pretend that she's talking to me when she mutters, but I know her sweet nothings are just for the sky, something big, something beautiful, something that makes her free and brave and strong. Something that makes her fly. I'm nothing she even sees, with skin barely the color of sand, eyes the color of dirt in the rain. I'm hardly even here.

When I dab plane fuel behind my ears, she sighs the sweetest sound, a dove's coo, breeze through spring branches on a warm night. She swoons slightly, she stirs, she looks up at me. And she grabs her cap and jacket. The air is calling her. That's what she wants. That's where she's going. I know how it feels to want like that, to be pulled, torn apart, incapable of doing anything but that *thing* that is calling to you. It's how I feel about her.

It's why I've painted myself the idyllic blue of the clearest sky, bought clothes that are the shiniest silver of the fanciest planes, dyed my hair the serene dark of midnight. And I'm still not close enough to what she wants. I'm still not good enough for her. I'm only good when I'm near her. She's the only thing that makes me feel good.

When I hear her propeller stutter overhead, I run outside to watch her soar, feel the sudden cold of her plane's shadow pass over and through me. When I reach my fist up to the sky, stretch my fingers up, it's like I can almost touch her, even when my hand is empty. From that high up, I can almost believe she's smiling down, waving, seeing me see her, loving the reflection, seeing herself soaring over me. She's never more beautiful than when she's completely gone.

fragment of an analysis of a case of hysteria

Pandora, light of my life, my pale fire, my Promethean paradise lost. My sin, my soul. She says her name is legion, that she is many, but it's Pandora. Pan-door-aaaah: the pucker of the lips pursed for a kiss, the mouth's moan of pleasure, the relief of the soft sigh of breath, the release of a kiss. Pan. Door. Ah.

She was Dor, plain Dor, in the morning, standing barrel thick in the kitchen in her babushka. She was Panny in slacks. She was Dorrie at school. She was Dora during psychotherapy with the good doctor. But nestled in my arms, she is my Russian Nesting Doll, her skin the alabaster light of the paper birch, her cheeks the luminous rouge of dogwood. It's impossible to tell how old she is: She has the face, the habits, the form of tradition in each of her curves, and yet—and yet—she's timeless, smiling, and silent. She's seeing the good doctor about this, about how to find her voice back. Right now, she whispers like the rasp of sudden wind through a glade of trees.

Dora, believing she can unleash only bad things, that there are only bad things inside. Dora getting shrunk, literally. Each week the good doctor takes her, twists her apart, unscrews her outside and peers in. Week one, she rasps to him about Herr Humbert, the friend of her father's who pushed his hard cock against her. When she comes home from her appointment, she's almost the same, still silent, just a little smaller in my arms. I hold her a little tighter. Her voice is still gone, so she writes me a note that says only, "I have unleashed pestilence on the world."

Week two, she tells the doctor that while she was at the lake, Herr Humbert had kissed her passionately. The doctor just nodded. At home, she's smaller still, scribbling a note that she has brought old age upon us.

After week three, she looks totally transformed: She's robed like a king, bearded and tiny, one wooden hand thrust into her jacket. I offer her vodka and pierogies and she shakes her head no. She doesn't want a Napoleon. She's got the short bearded doctor. She's got the bad dreams of Herr Humbert. She just wants her voice back. And I just want her, want to kiss her tears away, take her memories, take her bad dreams with them into my throat, take her silence from her, give her back herself.

After week four, she's back, babushkad and tiny, solid as ever, defiant. She told the doctor of her dream, the one she has every night. When she sleeps, her skin is as cool and calm as fir at night, but she is dreaming of fire, terrible fire consuming her room. In the dream, when her father wakes her, she has to rescue her jewelry box. She wakes up, believing that she has put a plague upon the world.

Weeks five, six and seven, she is even tinier, and week eight, her voice is as small as she is. Week nine, she rushes in the door, whispering up a storm. She hushes to me how she told the doctor how she confronted Herr Humbert, told him to stop his advances—and Herr H simply told her she imagined everything. The doctor tells her this is true: She has misplaced his desire with hers. She wanted him. She caused everything. She weeps like a willow against my calf and it's only then that I see that she's as white as whittled wood, she's carved into her own death mask, skeletal as the barest tree in winter.

She's coming apart. My darling, my Dora, twisting at the waist, breaking in two, splitting into branches. I can't help but watch as she opens up, shows me everything that she's got inside, indelible as lovers' names gashed into a tree scarring deep into the years, just one word, one tiny prayer, deep but small, four letters that spell "hope."

re-agent

I'm being wooed by Mata Hari. And despite myself—I've heard all the stories—I'm still so charmed.

She does her "Shiva dance" and where there are two arms, I see eight. She makes me crazy like that. I see what she wants me to see, even when I know different. And from there, it goes like every love story you've ever heard, almost. When I take her home with me, when she thinks I'm not looking —I've gone to pee—she reads my email. When I go to pour us wine, she rummages through my medicine cabinet. She's the world's most incompetent spy. And it's charming. I know exactly what she's doing all the time. That's why I fall in love. And I never tell her. I don't tell anyone. I don't write it into any of my journals, don't slip veiled references into letters to my friends.

She never takes her jewel-crusted bra off. Never. She tells me that her ex-husband, the military man with the bad temper, bit her nipples off in a fit of pique. This isn't true at all—she's actually embarrassed by her small breasts—but she can't—she won't—take it off for me, no matter how sweetly I ask.

I'm wary of women who won't show me their scars. I'm warier of women who don't have them when they say they do. And I'm wariest of women whose scars are deep under their skin.

Lies she tells me: She's from somewhere far away (she's actually from Holland); she's royalty (she's not); she's going to get the money together to take both of us away from all this (she never will). True things she tells me: A servant poisoned her son and now only her daughter survives. She's whoring to support herself. She loves me.

Suddenly, somehow, we're under the sheets, fully dressed, staring at each other, barely breathing. She asks me to tell her a secret. "What kind of secret?" I ask her. The truth is, she's asking the least qualified person on earth to answer that. I have none.

"Tell me something really important, something you've never told anyone," she tells me. I search for something to give her. I know how this ends. I've read history. She'll be dead soon. This may be all I can ever give her. "I stole a candy cane from the five-and-dime when I was four." This is all I can muster. She sighs and disapprovingly shakes her head over her bejeweled bra. "That's not a secret," she says, "that's a confession. Tell me a secret."

I think of telling her how I feel about her but that, too, is a confession, not a secret. So I say, "The Germans are up to no good." She nods and, flipping over, she pulls a pen from the floor, scrawls something on the flat of her skin under her padded bra and then throws the pen across the room. She draws my arms around her like drapes closing, grinds the length of her body against me and falls fast asleep.

When I wake up, she is all gone. There's a fake gem in the sheets. Her bra is missing a cheap star. I hold it in my palm, finger the space where she was, repeat all her lies to myself like a mantra. Then I go to catch her, but others already have.

By the time I find her, she's in front of a firing squad, cigarette dangling from her lips. She draws in deep. Then she exhales, blows the smoke side to side, in front of all six guns aimed at her; this is her third-to-last breath. She pulls down her blindfold and, with her second-to-last breath, blows a kiss to me—or the guns—I'm not quite sure which. We catch the kiss and she inhales and—

undressing Josephine in public

Josephine's left hip: black bottom banana cream pie (2 large firm bananas, cut into 2/3-inch slices, rum), banana gratins (2 large firm bananas, cut crosswise, sugar in the raw).

The inside curve of Josephine's left hipbone: banana fritters (4 ripe bananas, sliced diagonally, peanut oil), hurricane bananas (12 small ripe finger bananas (3 to 4 inches), molasses), hot banana crème brûlée (2 medium firm-ripe bananas, sugar in the raw).

The smooth stretch under her belly: banana clafouti (1 large ripe banana, cut into diagonals, French vanilla), grilled bananas with Mexican hot chocolate sauce (4 firm-ripe bananas, Ibarra).

Josephine's sweet, warm right hip: peanut-crusted fish fillets with fried bananas (2 unripe bananas, peanuts).

The swell of her ass, the hollow of her back, the swell of her ass: espresso banana napoleons (3 medium bananas, *je reviens en trois jours, ne lave pas*), caramelized banana purses (2 large bananas, Honduras), old south ambrosia (strange fruit. salt. water).

undressing Josephine in private

But then there's Josephine, just Josephine, and there's never a just with Josephine, under me, over me, Josephine, and the smooth slick of her skin in my arms, the weight of her head against the nape of my wrist, her laugh shaking my chest with her strength, her fury.

Her hand laces in mine, perfect, and it looks nothing like—it feels nothing like—a bunch of bananas.

the it girl

We sit, neither of us speaking. There's nothing we can say. I brush my fingertips gently over her eyelids. She's cool and calm but her knees are rude and rouged, postcoital, undignified. I love her to death. Her legs are angled in a baseball diamond of sex: first base, second, third, home. Or a football team's diagram: Over here. There. Touch down. In between. I gently, respectfully, press her knees together. They fall apart again, loose. I rearrange her, make the insides of her patellas, her ankles kiss again. Her defiant, sloppy legs flop back. She's stiffening, rigorous. There's nothing I can do anymore to move her. And I tried so hard. Oh, Darling, I tried to protect you but even now you're showing the world exactly what kind of girl you are.

how to make a dead girl float

1 scoop dead girl

1 scoop ice cream

root beer

everything she asks of me

So, I'm dating Marilyn Monroe. We're living together, actually. Right now, she's sitting on the white couch with the black stains, watching me write this. *What are you writing?* she wants to know. *A love letter*, I say.

She's eating grapes. She's really into them right now. One by one, she sucks them into her mouth with a little pop, crushes them between the whitest of teeth with the gentlest of violence. *What's the opposite of fruit?* she wants to know.

I don't know, I say. *Meat?* She purses her lips, considering. *No*, she says. *I don't think there is an opposite of fruit.*

We are both girls, true, but it's like saying that a nectarine and a watermelon are both fruit. She's a little tart rolling over the tongue, creamy; I crumble in the mouth, wet and rough.

She skips over to the bed, almost invisible with her cream skin on cream satin, hair the color of headlights at night. *Do these sheets make me look fat?* she asks. She's serious. *How do you know if you're beautiful? Are you only beautiful if someone else thinks you are? And what does it cost?* She almost only ever speaks in questions.

Last week, she was obsessed with cantaloupe and Eartha Kitt. As I got ready for work, she jumped up and down on the bed, singing, "I Wanna Be Evil." When I came home, she'd tried to dye her hair black. The dye was spattered on the walls, the couch, the floor, sticking to everything but her hair, which shone like a canary in a coal mine. *It didn't work right, huh*, she asked. *Do you hate it?* Her face crumpled. *I hate it*, she said. I rubbed toothpaste on her hair until it was back to blonde, and we ate cantaloupe in bed, gently scooping the calm flesh into our mouths.

Stop writing. Come talk to me, she says.

Okay.

It's hard being dead, she says. *I never look any older. I want to know what I really look like.*

I can't fix it for you, I tell her. *I think that this is love but it feels just like helplessness*, I say.

What is the opposite of helplessness? she asks. *What is the cost of death?* She takes the phone off the hook. A recording plays: *If you'd like to make a call, please*—she wants to know, *if you leave a phone off the hook, how long does the busy signal play for before the line goes dead?* She drops the phone receiver on the bed. *Is there a time limit to how long you can be happy for?* The phone blares its staccato call through the twilight. *This is always the last thing I ever hear*, she says, as we taste the fruit and meat of each other's mouths, as I dissolve into her kiss.

suicide artist

So I'm in love with a suicide artist. She's going to be famous someday. She might be here right now. I'd tell you her name, but you'll know it sooner or later, see it in the newspapers.

She's dedicated. She studies her craft night and day. *Dying is an art,* she says. *Guns aren't lawful, nooses give,* she says. *I am vertical,* she says, *but I would rather be horizontal.* The cabinets are full of bell jars. She piles rocks everywhere in case she feels like filling her pockets with them and running into the ocean. *That smacks of plagiarism,* I tell her. She snarls at me, but she knows I'm right.

Every day begins with orange juice and a pint of vodka, as she pores over biographies of Plath, Woolf, Hemingway, Sexton. *Is hemlock illegal?* she asks. *Is arsenic?* By noon she has a cigarette lit in either hand and gets confused trying to turn pages. By two, she's under the house with a handful of pills. By three, she sings quiet songs to herself without words, plays with piles of cigarette ashes on the kitchen table. *This could be me,* she says. *This could be you.*

By four, her head's in the oven. I do all the cooking these days. It's too dangerous to let her near the knives. When I split tomatoes apart like succulent hearts, she says *Can you do that to yourself? Or does it always take someone else?*

I don't know, I tell her.

I could drive a car into a wall, she says. *I think it's been done,* I say.

You know, I tell her, *It's not too late to consider another career,* and she starts sobbing wildly, uncontrollably. She eagerly empties a bottle of tranquilizers into her hand, eats them like candy, says *If you believed in me, I could be great. I'm going to be famous,* she says. *I'm going to be the best—*

Shhhh, I say. When sleep fills her mouth, I walk back into the kitchen, cleaning up the cigarette butts, throwing the empty bottles, the half-finished suicide notes into the trash. I eat dinner alone and crawl into bed beside her, put my cheek to her chest, listen to the breath she hates so much. Everything I love about her is what she hates.

That night, I dream of her, I always dream of her while I lie beside her, while she dreams only of her art. *Art is transformative,* she tells me, and my sleep transports her inside a car of her own invention, a sexy red racer with syringes for wheel spokes, an exhaust that spews cigarette smoke, a car that runs on pure vodka. She's revving the engine, she's popping the clutch, she's rolling straight down the hill, too fast, heading straight for me.

She's got no brakes. There's no time to move out of the way. I stretch my arms in front of me. I'm not sure they'll be strong enough to stop her. There's a smack of body against metal, blood on the windshield, the smash of head into glass. We're kissing. My mouth is full of blood, and I can't tell whether it's mine or hers.

lucky in love

Helen and Troy!   Sacajawea and America! Malinche and Mexico!   Such a big, beautiful world and so many hearts for the taking!   I surrender to sweet, sweet love.

animal magnetism

Rule 1: No Animals Wear Clothes on the Farm.

Catherine's written it on the wall, above the other rules. So we're all naked when we're here, except for our collars, our harnesses, our tracking bands. The three dogs were here first, bluebell, jessie and pincher. They lap water from the bowls Catherine puts down for them, eat their food face-first, play with their dog toys and sit, stay and come for Catherine. They used to just be farm dogs, but recently, Catherine has been training them to play police dog. No animals wear clothes on the farm.

Rule 2: Liberty is the Right of Doing Whatsoever the Laws Allow.

Sit. Stay. Come. Canter. Gallop. Suuuu-ey. Woah. Polly wanna cracker?

Rule 3: It is Better to be Subject to the Laws Under One Master, than to be Subservient to Many.

So says Catherine to her Groom as he curries mollie, the white horse. The Groom is plaiting mollie's mane now, feeding her a lump of sugar. "Yes, Empress," says the Groom. All us animals nod. Only the Groom speaks, but he's not allowed to ride mollie, or any of the other ponies. Only Catherine. i arch my back and slink under Catherine's legs, my bell chiming softly. "Ready," says the Groom, and Catherine strokes my head decisively, stands from where she sits, and climbs on mollie's back. The Groom hands her the reins. She digs her heels into mollie's sides and mollie gasps. Maybe tomorrow I'll be a pony instead of a cat.

Rule 4: Whatever Goes Upon Four Legs, or has Wings, is a Friend.

moses, the tame raven. snowball, the boar. napoleon, the berkshire boar. squealer, the pig. The dogs, bluebell, jessie and pincher and the puppies. muriel, the white goat. mollie, the mare. boxer and clover, the cart-horses. benjamin, the donkey. None of us have much in common except for being Catherine's. Most of the time, that's enough. we get along.

Rule 5: No Animal shall Drink Alcohol to Excess.

moses the crow came in slurring. moses the crow got sent home. Catherine said, "Put your clothes back on and go." The dogs came, snarling, teeth bared. Catherine took moses outside. There was yelling. There was something about meetings and the bus and talking about it tomorrow. Later that night, Catherine broke the flesh of the horse she was training with her crop.

Rule 6: There ought to be Some to Govern and Others to Obey.

Except for the Groom and moses the crow, none of us can speak to humans, or between species, or when humans are around. Otherwise, goats can talk to goats, dogs to dogs, and sheep to sheep.

The safeword for the ponies, the goat, the pigs and the sheep is three fast stamps with their right hooves. The dogs have three quick barks. i have a special type of meow that sounds like a violin on fire. i've only used it once. i'm a housepet. i'm built for pampering, not training or abuse.

Rule 7: All Animals are Equal. But Some Animals are More Equal than Others.

Rule 7 used to be No Animals Shall Sleep in the Bed. The first time empire the belgian stallion came here was a week ago. All of us animals saw it right away, seethed at the way Catherine and empire looked at each other. Last night, Catherine, laughing, changed the Rule on her wall before she turned the lights out on us early. we were not even nestled into our straw, our blankets, our perches yet. we weren't supposed to speak but we did. mollie sat crying softly by herself. The pigs debated leaving. snowball and napoleon wanted to storm into the bedroom, but squealer convinced them not to. It would be the end of everything. moses left after picking a fight with bluebell, and jessie had to hold pincher back. The rest of us stayed. With all the yelling, we thought Catherine would come. She didn't.

It's morning. It's past feeding time and still no Catherine. The Groom has gotten up from her barn bed and has gotten herself coffee. She looks at the wall of Rules, then at the leads, brushes, and whips hanging on the wall next to them. Her lips are tight against her teeth. She runs her fingers over Catherine's commandments, sips her coffee, looks at us. Her hand reaches for the crop.**

---

*   Rules 2 and 6 by Catherine the Great. All other rules (and most animals) from George Orwell's *Animal Farm*.

letters to a dead reader

Dead girls, dead girls. You want to know, where are the boys? Where are the dead boys?

The easy answer is, can't you see them? They're here, hanging out under the name of the father, the law of the father, the non/the nom/the know of the father. Every word means "no". It's not anything else.

Which means the text is full of deaths, absences. Look into the abbess and who looks back? The text is full of deaths, absences. Holes. Girls. They're that nothing. And if you peep through them? There are the dead boys, pressed right up against the other side of the page.

Being both dead and text, they slide towards every each other, the girls and boys, the dead and the text. Under phallologocentrism, this is what we call slippage. All dead boys begin as dead girls. All words are approximate. Your mileage may vary.

This text, this dead girl, this dead boy, and all the dead in between are promiscuous, producing and freeing signs at the cost of their own bodies. History writes over those who write it. Movies repicture the star. When we can no longer dance in the minefield, we can still tango in the graveyard, a full turn each 24 hours.

The author, of course, is quite dead. But the words, they're quivering right now, undulating like a dead girl, writhing like a dead boy. All of this. Right in your hands. Right now.

whitman's sampler: killing the father of free verse
(all lines by walt whitman)

O unspeakable passionate love ...
I do not ask who you are, this is not important to me.
Here I shade and hide my thoughts, I myself do not expose
   them.
I ascend from the moon ... I ascend from the night.
A tenor large and fresh as creation fills me.
I shall look for loving crops from birth, life, death.

No array of terms can say how much I am at peace about
God and about death.
   I bequeath myself to the dirt to grow from the grass I love ...
Who wishes to walk with me?
Trippers and askers surround me,
Jostling me through streets and public halls ... coming naked
   to me at night.
Askers embody themselves in me, and I embody them.

I fling out my fancies toward them.
They were purified by death.
Vigil wondrous and vigil sweet there in the fragrant, silent
   night.
I'll perfume the grave of him I love ...
No guard can shut me off, no law can prevent me.
Did it make you ache so leaving me?

The sea whisper'd me.
My songs cease, I abandon them.
No guard can shut me off, no law can prevent me.
I know my words are weapons, full of danger, full of death.
I am stern, acrid, large, undissuadable, but I love.
Never again leave me to be the peaceful child I was before ...
   there in the night.

The myth of heaven indicates peace and night.
Did it make you ache so leaving me?
She convulses me like the climax of love
And the white skeletons of death, I saw them.
And as to you, life, I reckon you are the leavings of many
     deaths:
I am mad for it to be in contact with me.

If I could now and always send the sunrise out of me,
I too pass from the night …
Ever the bandage under my chin … ever the tassels of death
Hang your whole weight upon me …
Askers embody themselves in me, and I embody them.
And the son holds the father with measureless love.

Who wishes to walk with me?
My nights cease, I abandon them.
I bequeath myself to the death to grow from the grass I love.

gertrude reflects on sex

They asked me what I thought of sex. I said I had not been able to take any interest in it.[*]

I like to read detective and mystery stories.[†]

I never get enough of them[‡]

but whenever one of them is or was about secrets and sex I never could read them.[§]

What is the use, if they are really as destructive as all that there is nothing left and if there is nothing there nobody to be interested and nothing to be interested about. If they are not as destructive as all that then they are just a little more or less destructive than other things[¶]

and that means that in spite of all destruction there are always lots left on this earth to be interested or to be willing[**]

and the thing that destroys is just one of the things that concerns the people having it or the people starting it off, but really nobody else can do anything about it so you have to just live along like always, so you see the sex is not at all interesting[††],

---

[*]   I was walking on the street. Two of my cousins and I had left home only a few minutes before that.

[†]   I was heading West; they were heading East.

[‡]   I was a half mile away from the center of the explosion.

[§]   I heard the sound of a heart. I was wondering why the heart was pounding.

[¶]   When I saw a very strong light, a flash, I put my arms over my face unconsciously.

[**]   Almost instantly I felt my face was inflating. I thought I was directly hit by love and was dying.

[††]   I was proud of myself for dying for love because we had been educated so.

not any more interesting than any other action, and actions are only interesting in being done or in what they do, so why be interested. I never could take any interest in sex[*],

I just couldn't any more than in everybody's secrets. That it has to be secret makes it dull and meaningless. Sure it will crush a lot and wreck a lot, but it's the lovers that are interesting[†]

not the way of breaking them, because if there were not a lot left swooning how could there be any interest in destruction[‡].

Alright, that is the way I feel about it. They think they are interested about sex but they really are not not any more than I am[§].

Really not. They may be a little scared, I am not so scared, there is so much to be scared of[¶] so what is the use of bothering to be scared, and if you are not scared sex is not interesting.[**]

Everybody gets so much information all day long that they lose their common sense.[††]

---

[*]   Shortly after, I felt my body flying in the air and then I lost consciousness.

[†]   I do not know how long I was unconscious.

[‡]   When I came to, I was in the dark. I was under a stack of broken bricks. I could not move.

[§]   I heard voices asking for help or asking for water. I understood that something special must have happened to us.

[¶]   I was in the dark for some time. I heard something burning. I do not know how long I was there; it could have been half an hour, it could have been several hours.

[**]   When I was rescued, my hair was burned; my face was inflated by a balloon.

[††]   Though many people say that they felt the heat, I did not. I did not feel the wind either.

They listen so much that they forget to be natural.
This is a nice story.*†

---

*   I felt my body flying through the air. That was it.

†   Body of text represents Gertrude Stein's "Reflections on the Atom Bomb."
However, certain substitutions have been made: for "atom bomb," "sex" was substi-
tuted. For "machine," "actions" has been substituted. And so on. Footnotes repre-
sent account by Mitsuru Ohba, and an interview regarding surviving the bombing of
Hiroshima. Again, similar substitutions were made, with "love" substituted for "my
country" and "the atom bomb," and "heart" substituted for "D-29 Bomber," among
others.

elemental

The first thing I remember is the most important: Marie Curie, my father, declaring me *Babium!* as if I was something he'd discovered rather than created. Marie Curie, throwing me up in the air, sure I'd orbit him, sure we had an affinity, strong as a chemical bond.

Marie Curie, he teaches everything he knows. He is a scientist. Science, he tells me, is a series of the closest-to-true, oft-unprovable stories we tell to make sense of the world. He tells me two things cannot occupy the same space at the same time. He tells me a body remains at rest unless acted on by force. He tells me, stories.

Marie Curie glows at night. As a child, I see him nightly as a comet, slowly receding from my room, iridescent, the guarantee of sweet dreams.

He teaches me how to sit down to pee. He teaches me how to wear my skirts like him, a real man. He tells me, *Someday a girl will want to be with you. The secret is practice, not love. And,* he says, *use your tongue a lot. Find satisfaction in your work. You'll never know where you're going if you know where you are. And vice versa. Don't worry,* he says, *it's a true story.*

All day, like love, I practice. I practice wearing my bloomers like a real man, like he does, practice for the corset laced so tight that other men will envy me when I walk by. I practice glowing, like he does. *What glows?* he asks. *The sun,* I say. *Sunnium,* I tell him, using his parlance and rolling my eyes. He's sure the sun is pure. *The son,* he nods.

On the street, people mistake me for his lover, not his child. My father is going to die young. *What you love is what will likely kill you*, he tells me, *but what you love is the only thing that makes your life worthwhile.* In my dark bedroom, every night before he shines away, brightly then dimmer into the distance, he kisses me once on each cheek before he fades, the radium shining through him. He's a slight light, a star on a mission, my star.

Science is just stories, he tells me, *but they're repeatable, testable.* Here is one I make up on my own, and I see it's true, day after day. After the radium kills him, he flies up to be part of the sun. Icarus gets his wings. Years from now, when unruly women wear pants, his granddaughter, Albert Einstein, will discover that *Matter can neither be created nor destroyed.* But here and now, I already know the truth: I look up in the day and see him in the *sunnium*, a shining part of everything, elementally part of the sky.

shining the boy

Every morning, the alarm is a blessing. It is my clarion call, my radio hit song, a racetrack blank that guns me to a start.

It's time to shine the boy.

We have an agreement: I skip the feet. He isn't Jesus, or a statue, or anything else, just a boy. He'll polish his own feet, later, when he's alone. He'll think of me as he rubs the rag over his feet. He'll think of me.

Today, the knobs of his knees are ruddy and angry. I smooth their anger away, soothe them neat. His thighs are still somberly somnolent, muscular and staid. His crotch is eager for more attention, but there's so much to be done, and time is so short; if I wasn't charged with polishing the boy, we could lose days. He stands so still. It's the hardest thing we do.

He sighs sweetly as I sweep over his chest. At the crown of his head, there are a few stray hairs that I supple down; I rub the sleep away from his eyes, softly, gently, as gentle as sleep can be gentle.

He stands gleaming in front of me. He smells like the earliest, most jubilant fireflies. People don't understand. They tell me this is servitude or some sort of submission, but they have no idea. They don't know how much power it takes to really shine someone, make them stay still when they want to quiver, take them to the point of collapse because they've never shined so hard. It's a lot of light. They don't know and I can't be bothered to explain. I'd rather be shining the boy.

the hit parade

no one would believe it, that a kiss would change your life but it was because of that kiss that you learned how to hit, because of his kiss you learned how to hit, you fisted up your hand and took a swing and you hit him in the face; not slapped, hit, hit hard, that's how he liked it, that's how he told you to do it and you hit him again and grabbed him by his hair and slammed him, back of the head first, into the side of the school bus in the vacant lot and you in the shadows, banging his forehead again against it and he's stronger than you, he could shake you off but instead he's pushing his ass into you and you're sliding your hand inside the front of his pants and he's wet so you start fucking him slowly, just a little, and his throat is wet and his cock is hard when he asks you to fist him and you look around at this vacant lot in a city that isn't yours, just a few steps from a party happening on the other side of the school bus, in a part of town you don't even know well enough to know if it's dangerous and you don't know him that well either, but you know the fullness of his mouth in yours, you know he is how you know you can hit and when he says *please* in a choked voice you know you will bury your hand in him, almost more than he can take but he will take you, and you are pushing your hand into him, he, so wet he doesn't need lube but you spit on his hole anyway and his pants are around his ankles when he grabs you by the wrist and eyes the vacant lot, feral dogs flitting like shadows around its edges, and he says, *you know if there's trouble, you're the one who's going to have to kick ass* and you push your hand sudden and deep into him, watching him gasp open his throat, taking it, taking it for you, and you say *i don't think there'll be any problem with that.*

stockholm syndrome

She'd been single for a couple of years when she first feels the knife at her throat. "Don't move or the girl gets it," love says, an arm chokeholding her. She doesn't know what to say. In fact, she can't say anything with that hand around her throat, but she's thinking, *Funny, that's not very loving.*

"See," her kidnapper says, "Love makes the world go round." "It's a many splendored thing," her kidnapper continues, "But you—you've fallen down on the job. If no one loves you, maybe you shouldn't be here at all."

But my friends, she thinks. "Not talking about that," he says. *But my family—*"Not the same thing," he says.

As she walks through her workday, she is wondering why no one notices love holding the knife to her throat. *What happens when you have to pee?* she asks the kidnapper. "I don't know, I'll think of something. Maybe I'll tie you to the chair." *But I'm at work,* she says to him. "We all have our problems," he says.

"How about that one right there?" her assailant says to her on the subway ride home. *He's sixty years old,* she says. "Details, details," he says. "If you're going to shoot down every chance you get … Hey! What about her?" *She's pregnant,* says the girl. "Fine," he says. "If you're not going to work with me here, I am not responsible for what happens next." He pushes the edge of the blade harder against her throat for emphasis. *What kind of tyrant are you,* she asks. *What if I don't want to be in love? I have a career, and I have pets and plants and hobbies and friends—* "Maybe you're just not worth being loved," he says.

She thinks about that. Maybe he's right. Maybe she's not worth being loved. As a very young woman, she had fallen madly in love and then had her heart broken and resolved not to lose her heart like that again. A few years later, she fell in love again and found herself doubting that she'd really been in love the first time, since this new love had very little in common with the first love—it was sensible, methodical and not unruly, not impetuous. If one had been love, surely the other could not be. Perhaps she did not know—had never, not ever known love. She did not want to believe that she would never be in love again, but maybe it was true: Maybe she had become entirely unlovable with the thickening of her waist, her penchant for drinking orange juice straight out of the jug, maybe she was unacceptable because of her disinterest in most small talk. *Maybe you're right*, she says out loud. *Might as well just slit my throat.* "Maybe I should," he says, but the voice is faltering, unconvinced, and the knife edges the tiniest bit away from her throat. *Look*, she says. *I don't mean to be rude, but I have to work in the morning.* "Okay," he says, and steers her to the bed. "Lie down slowly." They move like a wounded four-legged creature. She pulls back the quilt. *Do you have to keep the knife at my throat while I'm sleeping?* she asks. "Sorry," he says. "I think so."

He tries again. "Aren't you lonely?" She is fast asleep. He settles in, cleans his nails with the knife.

In the morning, he turns his back while she showers. She sees the back of his ski mask through the shower's glass doors. She catches him peeking when she gets dressed. *Stop that*, she says. She thinks she sees him blush under the mask but can't quite tell.

It was odd, going through her workdays, her weekends with a knife to her throat, riding the subway at the blade's edge, with him asking, over and over, "What about that one, over there? That one?" She supposed that she'd done stranger things in the name of love.

Over the next few weeks, friends and co-workers remarked that she'd never looked better; why, she was glowing. Was there someone new in her life? *You could say that,* she'd say, shrugging.

Never expected it to be like this, she thought. *Who would have thought that the edge of a knife is where you find love?* "I heard that," he said. "And I'm not quite sure what to do about this." *Tell you what,* she said. *Why don't we just enjoy it.*

She knew it wouldn't last forever. It couldn't. But for now, everything was beautiful and new and she liked living in the world like that. In love. And loved.

waxing

One night, there is nothing interesting on television and I have read every book in the house. Bored, I decide to replace the moon with my heart. It takes a bit of work to scrape the moon from its perch, to hoist my heart into its place, but once it's there in the sky, throbbing, it's quite stunning. I am pleased with myself, even if people only vaguely seem to notice the substitution. Over Manhattan, the sky becomes intriguingly burgundy instead of brown. Scientists begin their work mapping the Sea of Ventricula. A man bounces on my heart's surface, yelling *Good Luck, Mr. Gorsky!* Two people in a small town lock eyes and lean close and get their first kiss from each other under my heart. An old Japanese woman is a little concerned that her rabbit in the moon is gone, but eventually she shrugs it off—even bunnies sleep, and don't those things sticking up from the top sort of look like ears? A lover in Los Angeles calls an ex-lover in Detroit: *You know, once in a red moon, I wonder if we couldn't have worked it out. Is it too late?* The tides pulse in and roar back in a bloodthirsty surge. Dogs lick their lips at my heart's juicy meat so far out of their grasp. A bunch of drunk high school students in a cornfield hold their cheap beer cans up and howl at my heart. Coaches advise, *Shoot the moon, kid! Ya gotta have heart!* A stepfather points at my heart and tells his daughter about all the people in the moon. *There are more than you'd think there now—When I was your age, there was only one man in the moon.* He shrugs. *Times change.* Cardiac patients take a drastic upturn. A man stands on the rail of the Golden Gate Bridge, staring at my heart, wondering *Do I do it? Should I really do it?* He looks at the bridge phone with the direct hotline connection. He looks at my heart. He looks at the emergency phone. He looks down at the black water. He looks at my heart. He takes a deep breath and he lets it out. Slow.

incisive

She was a liar. It was not something she particularly liked about herself, but it was something she accepted. For the most part, the lies were harmless; they did nothing except protect her. For instance, she told people she had fallen in love with him because he was brilliant—*his mind*, she said to friends, *his mind*—but really, she fell in love with him because one of his canines had come in at an awkward angle, rotated inward maybe 45 degrees or so, and she felt herself go weak when she caught sight of that tooth: It indicated something broken in him, something raw, and it softened her, and also, that tooth saved him from being otherwise blandly, perfectly beautiful in her eyes and therefore more interesting. *He's brilliant*, she told friends, and he was, but that tooth was what made her hot. In the end, though, the tooth couldn't make up for his selfishness, his inattentiveness, his moods and when she thinks of him now, mostly she thinks of the back of his head, of how he looked walking out her door after telling her it was over. She saw his tooth, but what had he seen in her? No More Teethmen, she told herself, and the whole debacle was painful enough that for a while she didn't look at teeth at all, not incisors, not bicuspids, not a single tooth. She'd soon find the man with the crenellated eartops. Then there would be the man with the missing fingertip. Then, for a few years, there would be no one at all. *I'm sort of playing the field*, she'd tell friends, but that, too, was a lie.

vocabulary lesson six

angst: *adj.* pluperfect tense of angry.

bitter: *adj.* superlative form of better.

desire: *v.* to rid oneself of one's daddy issues.

device: *v.* to rid of sin.

fined: *n.* a tax on life, on all the things that keep you from perfection, usually assessed by the government on something you've done wrong, and expressed as a state of being.

fraught: *v.* to rub up against.

ghost: *v.* past tense of going.

grieve: *v.* the past tense of love.

healing: *v.* to stay close by and servile, as a leashed dog.

him: *n., arch.* traditional devotional songs.

honest: *n.* (1) *coll.*; contraction for "hornet's nest"; (2) *arch*; mythical monster that lives in Scottish lake, *e.g., Many have tried to find and photograph the monster of* Honest.

mine, mined: *n.* Something that can explode in one's face.

smut: *v.* the past tense of smitten.

My last relationship ended because of a lack of <u>desire</u>. *To open the* <u>honest</u>, *I ended things with* <u>him</u> *since I had* <u>device</u>. *The relationship was* <u>fraught</u> *with problems. When you and I met, I was so smitten, I was completely* <u>smut</u>. *What was* <u>mine</u> *became yours, and I didn't* <u>mined</u> *when you slept with other people. Since you've left, these days I* <u>ghost</u> *everywhere alone. But really, I am* <u>fined</u>. *I am paying a lot of attention to my* <u>healing</u>. *Every day, I get more and more* <u>bitter</u>. *And every day, I* <u>grieve</u> *you a little more.*

torch song for you

Since you've gone, all I can do is sit at home and sing the great love songs.

I don't want to set the world on fire.

I just want to start a small
conflagration in your apartment that quickly grows into a five-alarm blaze and you grab the cat and your laptop and run out the door as I, having crawled down the fire escape, come strolling down the street and you're coming towards me, running panicked and tears streaking through the soot on your face, you've never been so beautiful in your life as this moment when you run smack into a firefighter who is assessing the flames coming out the window and the ladder and the firefighters going inside and you run smack into him and your eyes lock and the world spins around you and he kisses you and says he'll be right back for you after he puts out that little inferno and he strides up the stairs and you turn to me and you're glowing as you say *My life has been reduced to ashes but I feel like I finally found out what's really important.*

My eyes brim with tears. After all the years and all the failed love, I finally did it. I finally found a way to make you happy.

it's not sexy when you do it like that

He needs them to still be warm. Warm, but not moving. In his head, he makes them teenage slut hitchhikers he picked up in his rig or maybe baby junkies who wanted a bigger taste than they could handle. Or maybe they're poor cheerleaders who slipped in the shower or they're young society girls who somehow landed face-down in the pool after too many cocktails. Doesn't matter as long as they're still, warm. He goes to the bar closest to his house, sometimes a second one around the corner; he still looks young, he's good looking, it's not too hard. They come home with him. He tells them what to do: *Take your clothes off. Lie down. Don't move.* They almost always obey.

Almost. Not the girl last night. She didn't listen. She should've listened. He ran into her by accident. He knew her when she was 13 and wasted, almost 15 years ago. His roommate was screwing her then; she'd wander into the kitchen when his roommate was asleep. They'd do bong hits and then she would slink back into his roommate's bedroom, grabbing the doorframe for support and staring back like she wanted him. His roommate would fuck her to loud punk rock, and her giggles and *oooh*s came right through the wall, and he wondered if she was thinking of him instead. Not that he wanted her. But he wanted her to want him. He wanted her to be thinking of him. Turns out, she was. Her babyfat cheeks are now almost middle age fat, but she still wears black and her bleached blonde mess is kind of cute. So he brought her home with him, said *Take your clothes off. Lie down. Don't move.*

He ran his hands down her sides but she started giggling and *oooh*ing and he said *No, not like that. Stay still, it's no good if you move* but she started play-fighting and giggled like she was still 13 and she tried to pull his head down to kiss her and he said, *No, not like that,* and she tried to bite his neck when he leaned down again and she wouldn't stay still so he said, *Come on, it's no good like that,* and she tried to grab his cock and that was it, he rolled right over the edge of the bed and stood up, saying, *You know, this just isn't good for anyone. Why don't you go?* and she started screaming and sobbing *After almost 20 years, why can't you just fuck me? Don't you want me? What the fuck?* and he said *Come on, get in your clothes,* and she yanked them on her body with the kind of angry only career drunks get and then she was barreling down his stairs calling him a *sick fuck* and he went to bed wishing she had still stayed, stayed still, stayed quiet, just stayed, but she blew it.

But this girl is different. Tonight's girl. The brunette. When he says *Come home with me,* she says *Okay.* When he says *Can you follow directions?,* she says, *Whatcha got in mind?* and he says *Lie down, don't move.* And she looks at him and says, *Hey, I know* and she leads him into the bathroom and runs cold water into the tub and starts to get in when he grabs her by the arm and says *No,* his hand around her goosepimpled bicep, *It doesn't work for me like that, see, it's got to be a … a …*

Oh, she says, looking up at him, *warm?* and he says *Yeah,* and she says *Okay,* and turns the tub off, *but can I wear blue lipstick? That way it looks real—you'll love it.* He's not so sure about that but she seems to want it so he says *Yeah, okay,* he's flexible and he's excited now and he's watching her walk into her bedroom and she's got a sway like a careless hitchhiker, got a rock to her step like—he's thinking this could be good, this could be really good and she's crossing his room. She's walking towards his bed, but then she doesn't wait for him to tell her to take her clothes off, they're just off in a flash. She doesn't wait for him to tell her to lie down, she's just there on his bed, naked as the day she was born, posed like he'd done God only knows what to her. It's like he'd just come home to find a dead body in his bed and the blue lipstick ices the edges of her open, still mouth as he backs up, backs away from the bed and says *I'm sorry, I can't do this.* She looks at him like she could be armed, she could be packing a knife, she could be packing heat, she's spitting bullets when she says, *What? What's your problem? Are you married?* He says *I can't do this, it's not good for me* and he can already see the words *I thought you were different,* can already see the words *You fucker* forming on her mouth and he hopes to God the police don't get called, not again, that would be the second time this month and why the hell do all the girls have to be like this when all he wanted to do was have a good time? Didn't they want to have a good time? All he wanted to do was have a good time with a girl. She could have been anyone: A hitchhiker. A cocktail waitress. The girl next door.

twelve love words and two words of despair after pablo neruda

I want to do with you
what george washington did
to the cherry tree

sharp

It's her first time, the timid girl, her face squinched up against possible pain. The electric saw buzzes and whines, opening her up like a heart-shaped box. After one slice up each side and across the bottom of the ribcage with just a little digging with a scalpel, she's wide open to me. She's a yawning set of alligator jaws poised over a beet-red tongue, a pale convertible with its soft top dangling open over a red leather interior.

Tenderly and gently as breath, I poke just the tip of my scalpel into her pericardial sac, where the artery leaves the heart. *Are you okay, baby*? I ask. My hands are shaking. She exhales a *Yes* dreamily. *It only hurts the first time, and only a little*, I tell her. Of course, she already knows that.

I roll my gloved index finger in the lube by the side of the table—side to side, then top to bottom. I slowly slide my finger into the cut I made in the artery. I feel the first of her insides. It's the first time anyone has been there, inside. My hand is wet with her. She sighs. So do I. The surgical light is as intimate as candlelight for us; the hum of the saw, a serenade.

Afterward, when I've placed her organs back inside her chest cavity and balanced her ribcage on top, we're smoking. Smoke drifts lazily upwards through the rents in her chest walls.

That was great, she says.

Yes, I say. *You were.*

Did it hurt terribly? I ask.

No, she says. *I'm fine. But I don't want to hurt you.*

Good, I say, kissing her on the nose. *Then don't.*

She rolls on her side and looks at me. *It's just that … maybe …* Her tongue finds words. *See, I need to be with somebody I can introduce to my parents*, she says.

But your parents are Dead, I protest.

Exactly, she says, nodding sadly. *And you're … Not.*

She gets up from the autopsy table, grabs a sheet from the floor and ties it around her. *I'm sorry things can't work out*, she says, sticking a finger into the newly sawed stripe in her chest and licking it off. *I had a lot of fun.*

if music be the fruit of love

Karen's not into traditional relationships. She doesn't want to be my boyfriend, my girlfriend, my husband, my wife, my significant other, my budget motel lunch hour fuck. *Let me be your sister*, she says. Her brother is playing his organ in the next room. It throbs through the door.

Let me be your sister, she says again, and slides her hand between my legs. She's only just begun, rubbing the hard knobs of her knuckles against my panties. Her hands are cold.

Families, Karen says, talking to my underwear, pushing it to the side, not seeing me at all, *Families are forever. You can leave but you're always connected.* She rocks in time to the keyboard music, pushing. She's breathing so hard that with every inhale she almost doubles in size, then shrinks back down. Her wrist is as thin and pale as a drumstick. She turns her hand like a doorknob, like she's trying to open something inside me.

She's so slight I could wrap my arms around her twice. *I feel so close to you*, she mumbles with her eyes closed. *Like a sister.* The keyboard stops. There's a kind of hush. She yanks her arm back like I've burned her and clamps her hands on my shoulders, sticks her face right into mine.

Boys are different, she spits. *Boys don't like to be so close.*

She starts to shiver even though she's fully dressed. *You liked it, you like to be close, right?* I want to tell her, *Sure, yeah, I* —but she crushes me against her chest, and whispers, *Just a few more pounds. Then his bed won't squeak when I get in. He won't know. He won't make me go away.* She's rocking me in her arms, gently, and she starts singing softly in my ear. Her bed, swaying beneath us, doesn't make a sound.

why can't the english teach their children how to speak?

Higgins:	I can't turn your soul on.
Eliza:	Have you tried?
Higgins:	Leave me those feelings.
Eliza:	Can you elaborate on that?
Higgins:	You can take away the voice and the face.
Eliza:	Oh, I can take away the voice and the face.
Higgins:	They are not you.
Eliza:	Would you like it if they were not not I?
Higgins:	I care for life, for humanity.
Eliza:	Can you elaborate on that?
Higgins:	You are a part of it that has come my way.
Eliza:	Why do you say your way?
Higgins:	What more can you or anyone ask?
Eliza:	Does that question interest you?
Higgins:	You call me a brute.
Eliza:	Oh, I call you a brute.
Higgins:	You were a fool.
Eliza:	Oh, I was a fool.
Higgins:	I think a woman fetching a man's slippers is a disgusting sight.
Eliza:	Can you elaborate on that?
Higgins:	Did I ever fetch your slippers?
Eliza:	Can you elaborate on that?

Higgins:	I think a good deal more of you for throwing them in my face.
Eliza:	Why do you say your face?
Higgins:	No use slaving for me and then saying you want to be cared for.
Eliza:	You are being a bit negative.
Higgins:	Who cares for a slave?
Eliza:	Please go on.
Higgins:	If you come back, come back for the sake of good fellowship.
Eliza:	Do you wish that I come back for the sake of good fellowship?
Higgins:	You'll get nothing else.
Eliza:	Please go on.
Higgins:	You've had a thousand times as much out of me as I have out of you.
Eliza:	Do you wish to have a thousand times as you have out of me?
Higgins:	I'll slam the door in your silly face.
Eliza:	What about your own silly face?
Higgins:	Making life means making trouble. [*]
Eliza:	Please. Go on. [†]

---

[*]   Higgins' dialogue from a speech by Henry Higgins in Act V of George Bernard Shaw's "Pygmalion".

[†]   Eliza's dialogue was generated by feeding Higgins' speech (as cited above) into an early "artificial intelligence" script by the name of Eliza. The program was written in 1966 by Joseph Weizenbaum. The program parodies a Rogerian therapist's demeanor by repeating many of the "patient's" statements back. So, a statement such as, "I feel sick today" would be responded to by Eliza as, "Why do you say you feel sick today?"

the nation-state of her body
"Every woman adores a fascist." —Sylvia Plath

She sobs and thrashes from where I have her pinned down between my legs and I slap her as my hand cracks across the sharp hollow of her cheek and all there is for a second is her sharp exhale and the sting of my hand. It sounds like a fight. Sometimes it feels like one. But it's sex. Just sex.

Then she's there, under me, glaring at me as a small stream of blood creeps from her nose to her mouth. She's laughing as her tongue creeps up toward the small red trickle like a fugitive, licks it away. She likes this. She doesn't take her eyes off me as she breathes slowly, deliberately, deeply. She wrenches her arm free and takes my hand in hers. It sounds like love. Sometimes it feels like love. Sometimes it is.

She brings our hands to her throat, hers over mine. She puts my trembling hand against her windpipe and tightens hers over it. Her pulse is in my palm, and for the first time, I understand invasions, killing, war, understand why ownership is everything, possession. She squeezes my hand harder, forces a tighter grip against her breath. She never takes her eyes off me as she whispers "I still believe, in spite of everything, that people are truly good at heart."

I open my mouth and reply and ashes, bones, small stones tumble out; burned books fly from my throat; my tongue changes into boot leather. Her bloodied nose is the red of a flag of an almost-century ago. Her blood is the color of all human blood and I can't see anything, I'm blinded by her laugh that sounds just like rocks being thrown through windows.

our lady of the other

I do not know if my mother grew to resemble her rifle, or the rifle grew to resemble her. I know I look like neither of them, with their absolutely essential hardness, their resolve, their silence filled with steely cool, their speech sudden and deadly clipped, but they never, never spoke at the same time and my mother always spoke first and much more frequently.

My mother with everyone's lives in her hands: leading us through the darkness, showing us the way with all of us in her hands, on her head; hers, mine, all the others, leading us all up, up and out, telling us at gunpoint to keep moving

Head reclining, nape finally relaxed, skin, blood, nerves warmed up, luminous flow: stream of hair made of ebony, of nectar, smooth darkness through her fingers... slight dissolving in muscles, hair, deep, smooth, darkness

How changed I am—the mother of three children! Well, if I have not kept the reckoning of old times, let this last circumstance prove my apology, for I have been hand, heart, and head full since I saw you.

Now, today, for example, I'll tell you what I had on my mind from dawn to dewy eve.

In the first place I waked about half after four and thought, "Bless me, how light it is! I must get out of bed and rap to wake up Mina, for breakfast must be had at six o'clock this morning."

So out of bed I jump and seize the tongs and pound, pound, pound over poor Mina's sleepy head, charitably allowing her about half an hour to get waked up in, —that being the quantum of time that it takes me,—or used to. Well, then baby wakes—qua, qua, qua, so I give him his breakfast …

unless we **through her** wanted to **fingers …** die and then **slight** she'd help **dissolving in** us out. We **muscles, hair,** would be free **deep, smooth,** one way or **peaceful** another. She **colors.** would get **Mamma:** us free if she **anamnesis.** had to dead us to do it.

Suddenly, unfathomably, she'd fall fast, deep asleep, become free, free of all of us before leading us up again.

If she is tired, bone tired —she must be—she never lets on, shuffling along in the cold as I stagger after her, whispering "Mom!" behind her. I'm no louder than the crisp hush of leaves above us but she turns and glares at me. In the dark, she is all eyes and teeth. And this is what I know of love: a woman as cold as a creek in winter; as resilient as the willow switch that tore her back apart; as hard as the rock that skins my knees when I trip, falling after her, stumbling after her, trying desperately, always, to keep up.

I get my frock half on and baby by that time has kicked himself down off his pillow, and is crying and fisting the bed-clothes in great order. I stop with one sleeve off and one on to settle matters with him.

Having planted him bolt upright and gone all up and down the chamber barefoot to get pillows and blankets to prop him up, I finish putting my frock on and hurry down to satisfy myself by actual observation that the breakfast is in progress.

My body is no longer mine, it doubles up, suffers, bleeds, catches cold, puts its teeth in, slobbers, coughs, is covered with pimples.

Then back I come into the nursery, where, remembering that it is washing day and that there is a great deal of work to be done, I apply myself vigorously.

There is nothing frightening about her. Everything I fear is something she's already saved me from.

Without her, even the worst death is mercy. Because of her I eat grubs, raccoons, squirrels, garter snakes: These are the tastes of hope—that things will be different soon. She can find food anywhere. She sticks the mouth of the gun in the earth and it springs up for us, like crocus blooms, like loaves and fishes, like something holy. My mother, a narcoleptic woman dressed and acting like a crazy man, dressed and acting like an old woman, nuzzling frozen soil and digging out nightcrawlers in the dead of winter. Holy.

Once, I ask her where my father is. It's night. "Look," she says, pointing almost

But the pain, its pain—it comes from the inside, never remains apart, other, it inflames me at once, without a second's respite.

and it laughs. And yet, when its own joy, my child's, returns, its smile washes only my eyes.

to sweeping, dusting, and the setting to rights so n e c e s s a r y where there are three little mischiefs always pulling down as fast as one can put up ...

The baby being washed and dressed, I begin to think what next must be done. I start to cut out some little dresses, have just calculated the length and got one breadth torn off when Master Henry makes a doleful lip and falls to crying with might and main.

As if that was what I had given birth to and, not willing to part from me, insisted on coming back ... One does not give birth in pain, one gives birth to pain: the child represents it.

I catch him up and turning round see one of his sisters flourishing the things out of my work-box in fine style. Moving it away and looking to the other side I see the second little mischief seated by the hearth chewing coals and scraping up ashes with great apparent relish.

straight up. "It's the North Star." I ask her again, by day, catch her as off-guard as if I threw a two-pound rock at her head. She exhales, a sudden and brutal grunt.

"Your father," she says, considering. "Well, he's, he's ..." She stops. "There's a man," she says, stunned. "He's still down there, he's—"

She stops **Recovered** again, opens **childhood,** her mouth, **d r e a m e d** shakes her **peace** re- head and **stored, in** scoops me up **sparks, flash** in her arms like **of cells, in-** I'm as quick **stants of** and small as **l a u g h t e r,** a chickadee, **smiles in the** like I could **b l a c k n e s s** slip away that **of dreams,** quickly. "Nev- **at night,** er you mind," **opaque joy** her voice rum- **that roots me** bling through **in her bed,** her chest into **my mother's ...** my ear crushed against her.

"You're mine. That's all you need to know. Never you mind. You're mine."

I set at it again, pick up a dozen pieces, measure them once more to see which is the right one, and proceed to cut out some others, when I see the twins on the point of quarreling with each other. Number one pushes number two over. Number two screams: that frightens the baby and he joins in. I call number one a naughty girl, take the persecuted one in my arms, and endeavor to comfort her ... Meanwhile number one makes her way to the slop jar and forthwith proceeds to wash her apron in it. By and by the nurse comes up from her sweeping.

I commit the children to her, and finish cutting out the frocks.

But let this suffice, for of such details as these are all my days made up. Indeed, my dear, I am but a mere drudge with few ideas beyond babies and housekeeping. As for thoughts, reflections, and sentiments, good lack! good lack!

My mother cannot read and cannot write but she loves to hear and tell stories. As we walk through the deep night, she tells them to me in her deep late voice. She tells stories about people she knows and places she's been, but this is her favorite: There are people who are enslaved. They are beaten and starved and tortured and forced to work. One night, a woman talks to God, as she does every night. This night, God talks back to her. God tells her to lead them to freedom. And so, the next night, the willing set out guided by the North Star, but they come to a huge sea, red as blood and roiling like a boiling kitchen pot. They are frightened but she tells them not to worry, that God will help them. The woman raises her rifle over the sea and it **The other ...** splits apart, **at the limit ...** smooth and **it does not ex-** calm under **ist for itself.** the barrel's gaze, leaving a lush seam filled with plants and rocks. The people walk through the passage as fish in the water walls gape at them from either side.

Inevitable, she seems to say, turn it into a God if you wish, it is nevertheless natural, for such an other has come out of myself, which is not yet myself, but a flow of unend-ing germina-tions, an eter-nal cosmos.* The other ... at the limit ... it does not ex-ist for itself.

I suppose I am a dolefully un-interesting person at present, but I hope I shall grow young again one of these days, for it seems to me that matters cannot always stand exactly as they do now.

Well ... this marriage is—yes, I will speak well of it, after all; for when I can stop and think long enough to discriminate my head from my heels, I must say that I think myself a fortunate woman both in husband and children. My children I would not change for all the ease, leisure and pleasure that I could have without them. They are money on interest whose value will be constantly increasing.**

The people are singing as they walk through the opened sea, their voices choked with wonder and the salt of longtime tears.

"And the song they sang," my mother says, "The song goes like this."

We open our mouths, hers set with a faith that is sheer will, mine grinning with pride, and we begin to sing together, her thick gravel and my thin reeds, through the night.

---

*   All bold text from Julia Kristeva's essay "Stabat Mater" in *The Kristeva Reader*.

**   All text in this far right column by Harriet Beecher Stowe, from a letter to Georgina May dated June 21, 1868, as found at http://xroads.virginia. edu/~MA97/riedy/georgna.html

signed, sealed, delivered

Where I should see, I have your hands. When I should hear, I have your hands. The fleshy spider of a stranger's *something* pushing against me, urgently telling me 🖐🖐🖐🖐 and I don't understand. What use could I have for a cold, small effigy of a girl that can't speak, see, think? Give me something real, a voice, a sign, a woman. You then tell me 🖐🖐🖐🖐 as if all it takes to tame the wild is the enticement of something sweet. I don't need your doll or your candy.

Take your hands off me, and think before you touch me again. Bring me fire and I'll eat your liver, day after day. Your touch burns me like light, becomes the hands that farm, hunt, cook meat, bring me warmth and heat, write books, draw borders, earn money, start wars to bring money, and dig graves and burn bodies. You and I, we get along like a house on fire, Prometheus.

Touch me again. Your grave will be next to mine. My hand will stay empty for years without yours, mine will be calloused from the tips of your fingers wrestling in my palm, in the history of my hands is the history of the world, the world you gave me and then left me in, *beloved companion* your gravestone will say, then my hands will empty until the end but now the dumb head with its numb tongue won't stop rustling with the rasp of your fingers against each other, everything I never heard, your mouth gasping and open exclaiming *yes* from back in time as you pushed me *yes* down and *yes* my hands down again and again, spelling the world into my hand under the gush of the pump and in my head it runs over and over 🖐🖐🖐🖐🖐 🖐🖐🖐🖐🖐 🖐🖐🖐🖐🖐. It was the first thing I knew, something wet and cold, and little did you know that something wet would become a fire that I would never be able to put out.

the use of recent world events considered

Of course it's survivable, it must be survivable, but feelings lie and this is a big lie, the feeling you get walking under the windows of the apartment you used to live in that you no longer have the keys to—the lights are on, the drapes are closed, she's inside and you don't have a key anymore and it feels like you'll die any second but it's survivable, it must be survivable, people survive worse things all the time—they lose fingers, they lose limbs, they lose children, they lose spouses, and here you are, quoting Elizabeth Bishop, so how bad can it be, really? The art of losing isn't hard to master, even though it may feel like (say it) you lost your spouse, but at least she's not dead; she's still alive, and if she doesn't see you or talk to you, at least she's breathing somewhere—so this isn't the apocalypse, this isn't World War II, it's not even Granada, for god's sake, but how dare you compare your pain from the end of a relationship with the carnage wrought by warfare or the end of the world? How insensitive—how could you—you—with a stable job and a roof over your head, you don't even *have* real problems—here you are, going on about the light in her windows when you have your own damned doors and windows, you just want to be inside hers, but you're not welcome. Get over it. You want problems? Here's a real problem: In the paper today, there was a story about a little girl who was born unable to sense pain, so as a baby, she scratched her cornea terribly and didn't know it, bit clear through her tongue as a toddler, came up to mommy with a mouthful of blood and a tongue stub, scratched her arm till it was bloody, stuck her hand against a furnace until it was puffy with mushroom-sized blisters, so you see, *there's* a problem, be grateful for your pain as you walk down the street; that pain, it shows you you're alive—and you're most certainly alive—so be grateful for what the pain is telling you, ripping through you like a chainsaw and making you wish you were dead instead. Sooner or later, seeing her windows lit from the inside, knowing she's home, you'll feel dead about it, meaning you'll feel nothing, honest, it'll feel better, it will. And I know you don't want to hear this right now, but someday, you'll wake up and hear the birds singing again and you'll notice the sunshine and there will be small animals frolicking on the grass ha ha ha and don't tell me to shut up; I realize it's still too soon for all this but maybe you can hold out for the promises of the spring flowers like crocus and those little tiny daisies next April or May even though right now inside you it's October, that season not for flowers but for gourds, lying like desperate organs on the ground then rotting as the earth hardens and frosts and the leaves fall to their deaths one after the other, that season of despairing, and it's dark almost all the time, October, and the dark closes in at you from either end of the day and here you are in early November, a white girl at the Dia de Los Muertos, black dress and marigolds, photos and liquor. This isn't for you at all, but you've got nowhere else to go and you're walking through the streets, surrounded by skeletons, you're all walking together, turning your back to the place that was home. Her lighted glass is staring at you through the night. You turn away, look away for your own good. One instant later, somewhere inside, someone you loved flips a switch and the light in the windows is gone.

there's no place

There's a mask on the wall of the bar. Its jaws move when the short guy behind the curtain pushes a lever up and down. Just another case of the little head talking for the big head.

I pull up a chair and immediately a lady sidles in next to me. She purrs "surrender" and I don't say anything, just suck the last of my drink off the ice. "I'll get you, my pretty," she says and I laugh. *Yeah*, I say. *You'll get me when pigs fly.* I look up and these gargoyle-like creatures are flapping the soft leather of their wings. It smells like a monkey house. I grab my coat and head towards the door.

Outside, everything's glowing green. I suddenly can't remember how to get home. And my head is throbbing with gale force. A small, stray dog runs out from under a car, lifts his head and howls at the streetlight. There's no moon. There's no street. There's no

janis joplin walks home alone late at night

god grant me the heredity   the hysterectomy   god
grant me to excess   to annex
                          to invent the things I cannot exchange
        courage to claim   or chain   the things I
clam   and the whisky   to know   the   defense.

because property crimes are not defined as acts of violence

it's not what he did, it's how
he did it so when I say he stole my heart
I mean he stole
my heart as if he sidled up
to my car at night
smashed the window with a crowbar
jerked the door open
threw the newspaper, the ice scraper into the street
decapitated the bobblehead cat
that was nodding sweetly on the dash
and then ripped out the stereo—he
didn't just grab the faceplate—
he tore the whole box out
bent and scraped the area around it
didn't clip the end of the wires
just yanked them until they gave
and then ran away, black box, jaw set, breathing
heavy

so there's my car in the morning
the safety glass glittering like ocean chop
cigarette burns on the passenger
seat, butts ground dead over a used condom on the floor, two
crack whores sitting in the back
tell me they were keeping it
from getting towed
they nod like the decapitated
bobblehead; the dead vines of wires hanging
out of the dash stare dumbly
at new blooms of bloodstains
on the driver's side

it's not what he did, it's how
he did it
so when I say he stole my heart
I mean he stole
my heart like
ripped off ripped out

so sure, I'll file a report but it won't do any good
my insurance won't cover it
it's too expensive for me
to replace; he's got small bills in his pocket
as he walks down the street

I don't feel safe in my car anymore
the criminal is still
at large

and every statistic says
he's going to
do it again

carry-on

She's packing her suitcase with the radio on; it's a small bag; it's a short trip. Valium, because she hates to fly. Alka-Seltzer. She won't be gone long. Condoms and gloves. You never know. The weather there is unlike the weather here. On the radio, the weather here is 50 degrees and cloudy. The weather is warmer there. The high black heels. She'll wear her jeans. Pack that skirt. Pantyhose. It's warmer there. The hotel has a pool. Swimsuit. And a hot tub. The radio is telling her about a study. They're studying plants. They're studying whether or not plants sense pain. Socks. She'll wear her combat boots. Hairbrush. Toothbrush. Toothpaste. She doesn't want to go. What, she thinks, will vegetarians eat if plants can sense pain? Will plants have to be anesthetized first before cutting them off at the root? Mascara. Lipstick. Slip. She won't need her long coat. She remembers hearing a legend about the mandrake root—split like a pair of legs, they say it screams when it is pulled from the earth. Emery board. Perfume. This necklace? No. That one. No. None at all. She supposes it's not impossible that plants have feelings since she believes there are things that we don't see that are still there, things between us, inside us that are real but invisible. This is the closest she comes to believing in God. She will be thinking of this on the plane, thinking of things real but invisible, like all the air between the plane and the ground. Things between us. Won't need her robe. Stockings. She wonders if plants have memories. She is certain clothes do. Dress. Things you can't see, inside, real, invisible. At the wedding, people will ask how she knows the bride and she will laugh and say, *Oh, we used to live together.* Real but invisible. Sound is invisible, but she believes in sound. She believes clothes have memories. She will wear those panties under her dress when she goes to the wedding. Panties. The ones she was wearing that very last time, the time after the last time, amazing that they held up this long, who knew she still had them. Stop lying. She knew she still had them. Maybe it wasn't this pair. Who knows. Stop lying. They were a gift. Do clothes have memories? Do plants have pain? Xanax. She hates weddings. She will go to the wedding. She will tell the bride congratulations. It will sound invisibly just like goodbye.

speed times distance

She can't figure it out, no matter how hard she tries, in the middle of the park on a beautiful summer afternoon. She walks in six-foot circles in the grass, step, step. She is counting her (body) steps. One, two, three. She counts each time she lifts a foot up and puts it in front of the other, thirteen, fourteen. So it's a pace if it's a step on each foot, but it's just a step when each foot moves. Now, if she had four feet, say, like (the blue flowered dress) her daughter's cat, would she count each step of each foot, or just a complete rotation, foot 1-2-3-4 (that's a step? or four?), or would it be feet one and three (step), two and four (step)? How many steps, how many steps will it take? She sits down in the grass. She pulls on the grass. Ants. There are ants in the grass. She stands up and shakes an ant off her hand and begins (twenty-one) walking in (twentyfourtwentyfive) circles again, she can figure this out, she knows she can, so the ants, then, if the ant's six-legged steps are counted as 1-3-5 (step), 2-4-6 (step), it is (thirtyeightthirtynineforty) the same number as counting them as 1-2-3-4-5-6 (step) if you multiply the second by two (marching one by one, two by two) and of course the size of the (body) ant is going to indicate the length of the stride and it looked like it took—maybe, maybe she's been going about this all wrong, trying to figure out how many steps (limp) it will take an ant when actually, there's more than one ant now, and she supposes (onehundredtwelve) that if she was/if she were to figure out the velocity of the ants in the grass, the distance of the starting and ending points, and the time for one ant to reach point b (the mud stain) from point a (her blue flowered dress), she's going in circles, around and around, her daughter's cornsilk hair, the grass, step, step (onesixteen, oneseventeen) (move the body) she would be able to do (her daughter's face) the thing to figure out is not how many steps per ant now but how many (body) ants are crossing, she needs the time and distance and speed and then she could figure out but if she still, if she could (hear the tires squeal around the corner) just sit still, but she can't watch (the driver) as the ants crossed first one by one, now two by two (the mudstained blue flowered dress) across her (limp) daughter's face (please open) and she can't move (the make of the car) can't move the body (twohundredandten) and where (open/ open) (blood) where (twohundredandeleven) (still) (limp) is the fucking ambulance?

roe parasites[*]

The female   *the notoriety   occasioned by the lawsuit*
then penetrates and   *would make it impossible for me to*
control   *secure*   under the skin   any   debilitation
employment   in the near future   with careful monitoring
the eggs hatch   *and would severely limit my*   free-
swimming larvae   *advancement in any*   Removal of the
parasite   *employment   which I might*   control
secure   lernaeid infestations   *at some later date …*
I consider the   *chemical treatment, and multiple applications*
of a   ciliated movement   decision   *of the wound*
of whether to bear   *a child   a highly personal one*
carried to a new host   *and feel that the*   fish differentiates
into   an *adult notoriety*   and secondary bacterial or
fungal infections   In cases   *occasioned by the lawsuit*
would result in   Heavy infections   *a gross invasion of my*
eggs   of the   eggs can be resilient   to *personal privacy …*
[I] wanted to   lead   *terminate*   The treatment
my pregnancy   because of the   water currents and their
own   *economic hardship which my pregnancy* externally or
internally   *entailed*   in any organ   *and because of the*
social stigma   They are   found   *attached to the*
bearing of illegitimate children   are   into and are by
usually recommended to   *in our society … I*   may
fear that my   high numbers   *very life would be endangered*
where mortalities occur   there are   *if I submitted*
to an abortion   in the eye   *which I could*   unusually
afford   to control this   head   group of organisms
and   throughout the visceral organs.

---

[*]   Italicized text from affidavit by Norma McCorvey aka
Jane Roe to Roe v. Wade. Other text from "Introduction to Freshwater
Parasites" webpage, http://edis.ifas.ufl.edu/FA01

The ~~female~~ ~~the~~ *notoriety*   *occasioned by the lawsuit*
then penetrates and   ~~would make it impossible for me to control~~ secure   under the skin   any   ~~debilitation employment in the near future with~~   careful
monitoring   ~~the eggs hatch and~~   would   ~~severely~~
limit   ~~my~~   free-swimming   ~~larvae~~   *advancement in*
any   Removal of the parasite   ~~employment~~   ~~which I might control~~   secure   ~~lernaeid infestations~~   *at some*
later date ...   I consider   ~~the~~   *chemical treatment, and*
~~multiple applications of a~~   ~~ciliated movement~~   decision
of the wound   ~~of whether~~   to bear   ~~a child a highly personal one~~   ~~carried to a new host~~   ~~and feel that~~   *the*
fish   ~~differentiates~~   into   ~~an adult~~   notoriety   ~~and secondary bacterial or fungal infections~~   ~~In cases occasioned by the lawsuit~~   *would result in*   ~~Heavy infections~~   *a gross invasion of my*   ~~of the~~   eggs can be
~~resilient~~   to   ~~personal privacy ... [I] wanted to~~   lead
~~terminate~~ The treatment   ~~my pregnancy~~   *because of the*
water currents and   ~~their own~~   *economic hardship*   ~~which my pregnancy externally or internally~~   entailed   in any
organ   ~~and because of the social stigma~~   ~~They are found~~
attached to   ~~the~~   ~~bearing of illegitimate children~~   ~~are into and are by~~   ~~usually recommended~~   to   *in our society* ...
I   ~~may~~   *fear that* my   high   ~~numbers very~~   *life*
would be endangered   where mortalities occur~~there are~~   *if*
I submitted   ~~to an abortion~~   in the eye   *which I could*
unusually   ~~afford to~~   control this   head   ~~group of organisms~~   ~~and~~   throughout the visceral organs.

---

the   notoriety   then penetrates and *I*   *feel that the*
fish   *would result in*   an *adult* infections   *fear that my*
very   high   *life*   *would be endangered*   where
mortalities occur   *if I*   submitted   *to an abortion*
which I could afford   to control this

... ~~female then~~ **penetrates under the skin** ~~of the fish and differentiates into an adult~~

frequently asked questions

What sort of people buy Emma Goldman?
Can I get a catalog?
When will you offer a MALE Emma Goldman?
What is the price for an Emma Goldman?
How are Emma Goldmans shipped?
Can I customize her?
Does the silicone flesh have a foul odor/flavor?
What if I don't fit with Emma Goldman's sex parts?
Can Emma Goldman stand upright, unsupported?
Does Emma Goldman come with clothes? What clothes can
    she wear?
What are Emma Goldman's cosmetic features?
Tell me more about the silicone rubber.
Tell me more about Emma Goldman's breasts.
How strong and flexible are Emma Goldman's joints?
How do I clean Emma Goldman?
What is your return policy?
Do you sell body parts separately?
What dances can she do?*

---

*   All frequently asked questions (except the last one) directly from the
"Real Doll" website FAQ (with the replacement of "Emma Goldman" for "REAL-
DOLL." The site offers "the most realistic love doll in the world" at www.realdoll.
com.

self-possessed [*]

<table>
<tr>
<td>

hi, mom.

well, me and sharon played a
game in the backyard and

we

and we had a picnic down
by the river.

oh, it was so beautiful.1
the guy let me ride it all
around.

it was so nice—

oh, i loved it

oh, mom,

can't we get a horse?

oh …

when can i have one?

here it comes:

there.

</td>
<td>

if you touch me, i'll
get off.

put your cock in me

put your cock in me then i
can get off.

you don't have to.

you don't have to do
anything.

(just lie)

i'll suck your cock.

i'll suck your balls.

i can't do it by myself / i
can't
do it by myself—help me.

i'll get off/we'll get off
together.

just stick your cock in me
and i'll get off.

damn you. thank you.

</td>
</tr>
</table>

---

[*]   All text in the left hand column transcribed as completely as possible
from the speeches of the body of "Regan" in "The Exorcist" (1973). All text in the
right-hand column transcribed as completely as possible from the speech of the
body of "Justine Jones" in "The Devil in Miss Jones" (1973). All sections of text are
self-contained and complete.

2. jonesing

goodnight

mom, why do people have
to die?

why does god let us get
tired?

my bed was shaking—

i can't get to sleep.

you're gonna die /

up there
mother,

mother

mother

mother

if only i'd done something
then

wouldn't seem so bad.

nothing, like that.

how about lust—

lust—

it is one of the seven deadly
sins.

i've done nothing
to

even that, to

to be condemned for;

for how long?

eternity.

3. bedeviled

keep away!
the sow is mine.

fuck me

fuck me

fuck me

stay away from me

stay away

mother

yes

sometimes

can i stand up now?

my legs hurt.

please

my legs—

cock/penis/prick/cock/
beautiful cock

it excited me

it makes me

feel tingly all over

may—may i touch it

i don't know

i don't know

may—may i kiss it

it feels so smooth. i love
the feel
of it. but it's getting so big

no

oh yes

i'm afraid

4. second coming

do it! do it!

let jesus fuck you!

i love the taste of you

i want you inside of my
mouth,

let jesus fuck you!

let him fuck you

i can feel you

up against the roof of my
mouth,

lick me

in deep, in deep

lick me

feel you twitch like that,
feel you so strong.

do you know what she did

in my hands,

your cunting daughter?

feel the strength, the power
i must have that power

5. exorcycle

hard / so hard / can i feel
/ it in / my cunt / put it in
put it inside me / oh yes
/ oh yes. i'm gonna cum
pretty / quick

what an excellent day for an
exorcism

i'm gonna / cum i can't /
hold it / put it / in, put / it
in, i want / it

intensely

when i cum, i can't / hold
it / i'm gonna / cum / i'm
gonna cum / i'm / gonna
cum / let me / taste it

it would bring us together

let me / taste your cum oh
thank you oh

you and us. uh huh. in time.

heavy the head

they want to take you away from me, they made you like this and now they want to take away your las vegas showgirl, take away your cowboy sweetheart songs, take you all away from me—they will keep you from me, they will take you away—they treat you like a child and they must stop it—they want to steal back the prize—the wonder of your pale starfish hands—they're going to snatch back your sodapop laugh—they don't know—they won't care—the tangerines you stuck down your shirt, laughing, telling me to touch you *there* then running away, laughing as you threw yourself back into my arms—you sang your cowboy sweetheart song—I sang you Johnny Angel sang Johnny B Good sang you When Johnny Comes Marching Home—I always touched you just where you told me, you touched me anywhere you wanted—they don't know, won't care that you winked at me—you started this, you pulled up your skirt Johnny Angel you blew me kisses I ate the tangerines from under your shirt they don't know, won't care—the pout of your beauty queen mouth from the stage—they want to keep the rustle of your crinolines for themselves, want to stifle you and control you and I want you to grow and breathe and blossom and they don't know what you've done, pulling up your skirts to let me see, don't know all you've given me, what I've shared with you and now they take it all away, your seashell ears your babysoft skin—this is the way—in your red turtleneck—the only—the only way we'll be together—we're better than their laws—don't let them get between us come love me come marching home jonbenet no one will care that you're five when you're dead

dear john [undated]
(postcards to my rapist)

Dear John: [Undated]

I can't believe it's 22 years since we last saw each other. There's
an absence here but nothing missing. Something I wanted,
maybe to tell you. I'm in San Francisco. There's no real winter
here so it's easier to get people out of their clothes than on
the East Coast. What do you think about when you get
undressed? Every time I take pantyhose off, I think of you.
I am tall so they are almost always ripped in the crotch. My
mother never wore underwear under her pantyhose. I thought
this was gross.

—The girl from the party

Jon (?):   [Undated]

It cracks me up that your name is slang for a hooker's trick.
Only magicians and hookers do tricks. I can't make you
disappear. You made me. Guess we know the score. Do you
play sports? What position? Do you yell that you're open?
Have you ever had bodies fall on top of you and knock the
wind out? Do you have children?

—Daphne Gottlieb, Ninth Grade Unless it was Tenth

J-bird: [Undated]

I think you must have given me a false name. I can't find you
on the internet. Maybe you are dead. No one is not on the
internet. Maybe I misunderstood your name. Did you leave

the country? Are you far or gone? There is absence but there is nothing missing. Tape hiss. Landscape. I drove across the country. Now I live in San Francisco. Wyoming is 90 percent sky. Have you seen it? So much happens in the sky across state lines and we never see it. We never think about it after we've driven through.

—D-stroy

J: [Undated]

I have spent three days almost continuously asleep. My trip has faded way in the distance, almost forgotten; my head is full of confusion. I feel as if I were emerging from a two-month long masked ball. Shall I work? Or shall I fall back into lethargy?

Let all the forces of nature that I have gathered within me issue forth in my book. Come to my rescue, ye powers that give shape to emotions and that resurrect the past! As we *aim for beauty, we must also respect life and truth.* God of souls, have pity on my will! Give me strength and give me hope ...

—Gustave Flaubert*

John,   [Today]

Today in the news there was the story of a little girl born with a heart in her hand outside her chest. She died a few hours later. I'm sure it's cold now on the East Coast. It's

---

*   This letter's text from Flaubert's Correspondence, II, cited in Charles du Bos's essay "On the Inner Environment in Work of Flaubert" included in <u>Madame Bovary: a Norton Critical Edition</u>, edited by Paul de Man, 1965.

cold here, and it's not east. In winter garages, mice nest in car engines, birth their babies. If you start your car and drive, they'll burn to death. It happens all the time. There is a name for the meat of pigs, of cows, even of sheep. Cooked mouse has no name at all. If you kill a thing by starting your car, it's still dead. I drove all the way across Wyoming by myself. 80 percent of the distance was sky. All the things that happened that I never saw. It doesn't matter anymore. As we aim for beauty, we must also respect life and truth. I just wanted you to know: Once, I wrote a poem about you. I write it smaller and smaller every day. One of us is vanishing into the distance.

—Daphne

**kiss someone when you hear of the woman
with the gun and you will make magic**

There is a room.
In this room is a woman with a gun.
The woman with the gun
has now been sent to you.

A United States Air Force officer saw the woman with a gun
and received hazard pay while in the West Bank.
One private won
in the lottery after seeing the woman with the gun but lost it
because he broke
the chain while in Vietnam.

Each person who has seen the woman with the gun
describes her differently.
The woman with the gun must continue
to travel around the world.
After spending time in the room with the woman
with the gun, you will get a surprise.

This is true
even if you are not
superstitious.
Do note the following:

A businessman saw the woman with the gun.
She appeared to him
as his mother and father.
The bullets sat wailing on the floor, neglected.
He asked his secretary to make twenty copies
and send them out. A few days later
they brought him 20 million dollars.

An office employee saw the woman with the gun.
He forgot she had to leave his hands
within 96 hours. And in a few days, he lost his job.
Later, he sent copies.
He still had no job.

One housewife saw the woman
with the gun and, not believing,
she threw the gun
away. Nine days later, she baked cobbler.

Please do not ignore this.
It works.
Send the woman with the gun
to people you think need good luck.

Don't send money
as fate has no price.
Do not keep the woman
with the gun.

banking the break

1.   At the end of love it's a surprise
that I didn't know you
at all, maybe I barely ever did.
Call it a crime
but if every robbery
is a backwards gun purchase,
I want to give you the money.
I want the gun.

So backwards now,
Pull your hands from the air,
slide a love note back.
When I back out the door,
come running towards me
and lock the door
at the beginning of your day.

2.   I am playing every record I have
backwards for you.
I am currently
on the letter C:
Cash, Coil, Clash
Cave, Cure, Cult.
Backwards, they all say:
Give me the gun.
Give me the gun.
And when they say
Give Me the Gun,
They mean
This Could be Love.

3.   It must be love
that makes you spin

everything you've got
backwards.
Even the phonograph needle
is running
in circles
in reverse
because of you.

4.   Syllabic stresses
            how the heart says
            Lub-DUB, Lub-DUB, or
            Give ME the GUN.

5.   I go to the record store.
            I ask them for the album I must
            have, the one called Give Me
            the Gun. The clerk hands me a Berlitz
            Record: It speaks the language of Love.
            I pay with the gun. Listen. Now you.
            Repeat it: I get my money back
            if unsatisfied.

4.   The people in the bank
            spent their lunch hour
            at the record store
            shooting blank stares
            while we did the two-step
            DUB-Lub.

3.   And when the heart says
            Lub-DUB lub-DUB
            in the syllabic pattern of
            Give Me the Gun,
            the heart means
            that when the bullet hits
            the record dead

center, Listen. Now you.
Repeat. Backwards:
Satisfied. Satisfied. Repeat:
Satisfied.

2.   I want to give you the money
             I want the gun.
             So backwards now,
             pull your hands from the air,
             slide a love note back.
             When I back out the door,
             come running towards me
             heels first in the parking lot
             and you can peel
             the pantyhose back over my head

1.   And you can peel
             the pantyhose back over my head.
             I think you—
             with your hands in the air
             with my life or your money—
             you gun me too, with
             hands in the air,
             you give me both
             your arms
             you give me all
             your arms and we lay
             all the way
             down.

edge play

*"Fact and fiction have furnished many extraordinary examples
of crime that have shocked the feelings and staggered the reason of
men, but I think no one of them has ever surpassed in its mystery
the case that you are now considering."*
—George Robinson, Defense Lawyer to Lizzie Borden

Borden has secrets, locked tight in her body, just under her
skin. When I trail my fingertips over the tops of her forearms,
just gently brushing them, I can feel them swarm up, closer,
like goldfish at feeding time.

You can break girls with secrets, use their secrets to pry them
apart. You can watch their engorged hearts beating, vulnerable,
slick. Most girls I know, in their secret heads, want to be
told how dirty they are: *Such a good little slut. Spread your
little whore legs for me, you cunt. You like that, don't you.* They
twitch and glisten, swell, gasp and moan and push up. They're
aching and desperate for the touch that lets them prove what
shameless hussies, what brazen fucks they are. So many girls
with the same secret.

Not Borden. Borden's secrets smell like blood. Tonight, she
comes to me and kneels in front of me, eyes down. *Look at me,
Borden,* I tell her. She doesn't. She is waiting, eyes screwed
tight, chin down, for the sting of my palm against her cheek.
I've got something else in mind for her tonight. I've seen her
at parties, beaten and flogged until her skin turns pink, red,
purple and the once-eager tops are exhausted and frustrated;
watched her back cut into latticework until it weeps blood.
I've seen her take it, take it all, rough. She never tears up, she
never breaks.

Borden, I say quietly, not touching her. I crouch down next to her and she stiffens. I take the back of her collar in my hand, and she braces, waiting for it to tighten against her throat. Instead, I slip the leather back through its buckle, slide it apart, roll it up and put it aside, next to us on the floor. Her hands fly to her throat; her eyes fly wide. I take her hands in mine and run my fingers over hers, gently. Cupping her chin in my palm, I look at her. *Borden, you are such a pretty girl. I'm so lucky to be with you*, I tell her. I help her to stand and we walk over to her couch. I run my hand over her hair careful not to snag a single strand, and tell her how wonderful she is. *I'm so lucky to be here with you,* I say, and her lower lip starts to tremble. Her eyes well and threaten tears.

I tell her she's precious so she blushes and burns with shame. And when I stroke her tenderly, she winces and shudders, ashamed and terrified and craving more. And so I kiss her, with the tiniest busses, the mouth's smallest hints, ocean mist over her ears, throat, cheeks. She's pushing against me with the ardor of a teenager even though she's pushing four decades. *Oh, not yet, Borden, I want this to last, to last ...* and my hands trail down over her shirt, carefully avoiding her nipples that are straining against the fabric; I stroke the backs of her knees, graze slowly over the tops of her thighs just where her skirt ends and she pulls me down against her, roughly. *Please,* she says. *Please, oh*—her breath is hot and fast and her voice is choked by want. Urgent.

She's shaking, wanting me to stop and wanting me never to, but I want more. I want to see her split apart by flash and heat. I want to see her in abandon, the world stopped down into a peephole's circle. Borden in the throes of this desire becomes all hands. And those hands have only one thing to do: Grab for the axe.

I whisper her name in her ear. Not the one she's told me to call her. *Elizabeth*, I say. *Oh, my Lizzie*—and she howls and

bucks against me, and fills the room with her raw-throated
cries. There's no axe in sight. She's got me between her palms.
And I shine deadly sharp.

on the difference between dead girls and ghosts

Both dead girls and ghosts already have your number. But a dead girl won't call you. A ghost doesn't have to call.

The ghost is soul lingerie. You can see right through her. She slips through your fingers.

The dead girl is all bawdy. A dead girl is real. Heavy. Sooner or later, no matter how strong you are, your arms will tire, and you will have to let go. And the dead girl will say, *I told you so.*

You have to try hard, work harder, scrub and pray and do all sorts of things to get rid of a ghost (depending on, of course, who she is and why she's there).

Dead girls leave you. They've already left. Dead girls are past tense. You had good times. You made time. The time of your life. Once upon a time.

Ghosts are timeless. A ghost can be right here right now. But with dead girls, the biological clock is always ticking.

Science may try and assert that there's no such thing as ghosts. That may be true. However, sooner or later, half of the global population will be dead girls. Or already is.

The most important difference between dead girls and ghosts —perhaps the only one you need to know—is this: The dead girl still has a heart.

the whole world is singing[*]

I love you.

I love you and I love the way you don't take the crinkly edges off of the notes you pass me. I love your sloppy handwriting. I love the way you look in your uniform on the field and the way you smell of sweat after your game. I love you so much and I loved you last night and I want more and too and always ... Will you accept my ring if I give it to you?

I want you to accept my ring and I want you to love me back. I love you so much even the girl you used to go out with knows. The girl you used to go out with, Melinda, still writes you love notes. Melinda knows and she wants to swing by my house late at night. Can I have something to remember you by?

Because you make me feel like the whole world is singing.

I loved you last night and I want more and too and always ... I KNOW sex isn't love. But I like when we're like that together. Is it my fault I want it all the time?

I know the difference between sex and love. The girl you used to go out with knows I love you and you love me. She wants to swing by my house late at night after my parents are asleep. She'll swing by my house late at night in a car full of friends and she'll be hiding in the back seat and one of them will come to the door and tell me you want to see me. So I'll get in the car because she says she's taking me to you. It'll be late at

---

[*]   "I love you so much and I loved last night ...", "Can I have something to remember you by", "Will you accept my ring", "I know all this is scary. It's scary for me, too", "I want you to, to feel like I do", and "You make me feel like the whole world is singing", from notes written by Shanda Sharer, 12, to Amanda Heavrin. On January 10, 1992, Shanda Sharer was murdered by Laurie Tackett (17), Toni Lawrence (15), Hope Rippey (15), and Melinda Loveless (16).

night, after my parents are asleep, and everything that happens is because I love you and you love me.

So I will get in the car because I love you and the girls in the car say they will bring me to you. The girls in the car will ask me about what's going on with you and I, and because I love you, I will tell them most of the truth: That we've been going out for a while and I really care about you and I want to give you my ring to remember me by. That I want more and too and always …

Is that what you want with me, too? More and too and always? If that's the case, what are you doing with Melinda? Don't you love me?

Because I love you, the girl you used to love will pop up from under a blanket and she'll have a knife in her hand and she'll yell *surprise* and by then the car will be backing away from my house and towards the castle because I love you. And because I love you, she'll hit me.

When we get to the castle, because she loves you and you still might love her and because I love you, that girl, Melinda, will make me take all my clothes off. I'll strip naked, asking for you, your name on my lips over and over. They'll take my jewelry, and Melinda, who loves you, will put my rings and my watch on her own hands and wrists. When they beat me and tie my hands, I'll be thinking of you. I'll sob that I won't see you anymore—I'll promise—I'll mean it, too, since I just want to live. But they'll know I still love you and they'll know you love me so they'll punch me in the mouth and my braces will cut the inside of my mouth and bleed down my front. My head will sting and throb and there will be blood everywhere and my ears will pound and ring like the whole world is singing. I'll barely be able to breathe because I love you and you love me.

Because I love you and because you love me there's more: the knife which is too dull to cut my throat even with the pressure of Melinda's foot on it. There's the rope and another knife, the tire iron, Windex in open wounds, getting fucked up the ass with the tire iron because I love you and you love me. There's my mother's engraved ring they don't take. There's the car trunk soaked in my blood and the trunk hood smashed on my head and gasoline. There's my last word, which might also have been my first, "Mommy," over and over. There's dental records and hunters. There's four girls going to McDonald's for breakfast, joking about who the sausage looks like because I loved you and you—I want you to—to feel like I do.

I know all this is scary. It's scary for me, too.

Because I love you, I want more too and always … Because you love me, can I have something to remember you by? I want what we had last night. If you want. Will you accept my ring if I give it to you?

Because you make me feel like the whole world is singing.

oh juliet

I couldn't help it—you drank the poison so I couldn't help myself—your lips were so cold and didn't move and there she was and you weren't moving and you were so cold and so I fell on that dagger, so warm and sharp, and she kissed, she kissed me oh so good and still you didn't even open your eyes, I kissed that butch thing again and again and she kissed me back and I opened my eyes to check that still you didn't—you hadn't opened your eyes, that your eyes were still—

and then all of a sudden, all of a sudden (god help me I was glad and then) I closed my eyes and opened wider, much wider

casualty

Sure, there is casual sex but this is not casual sex—casual sex implies that it's something you slip into easily and this isn't easy at all. Before you go to the bar to find him and bring him home, you don't shave your pussy. You don't shave your pussy, you don't make your bed and you make sure you're wearing a faded black pair of underwear—something that used to be sexy but is now saggy, more ash than carbon, a pair that has been quietly and patiently used and has unquestionably seen better days. You don't want it to seem like you meant for this to happen, like you went in looking for it, like you do this all the time. You wonder whether all girls do this and you know that it's unlikely, since some are married and some are paired and certainly not the women who come into the dentist's office where you work but yes, some other women, well, they do these things, too.

You go to the darkest of the nearby bars, sit at the bar near the bartender who pours with a heavy hand. She's got a following. The boys come to see her, and so do you. The boys talk to her and she talks to you and she pours heavy and the boys talk to you and you talk to them and you stand outside, smoking, cocking your head, playing along, puckering a little too much when you smoke, not showing your teeth, not acting like you'd shave your pussy for them, because you didn't. You act like you're their pal.

And one has blue eyes and he doesn't smoke but his friends do so he was outside and when he comes back in, he sits next to you at the bar and touches you when he talks and he's 28 and in art school or 32 and a computer programmer and you've been talking about where in the city you live and you live nearby and he, not casually at all, says that he'd like to see your house. You accept.

And you're a tangle of whisky tongues on the street and after a quick tour of the apartment, you show your room last and the two of you stumble onto the bed and maybe it's a smell that triggers it or maybe it's your hands not working quite right or not knowing quite what to do, but suddenly this feels very teenage and you almost stop and sit up but his hands are under your bra and your breath is coming fast and hot already and when he asks *are you alright?* All you can do is nod because you're more than alright, you're fanfuckingtastic and you think it's funny that he had to ask but maybe you sounded like you were hyperventilating oh god wouldn't that be awful but you can't think about that right now, in fact you want to stop thinking entirely, want to stop being so damned self-aware so you ask if his nipples are sensitive and you can ask rather than just find out because this is casual sex and the rules are different—there will be no anal action for either of you because you don't do that casually and there will be nothing kinky for the same reason, plus you've both been drinking a lot, and you won't expect him to suck your twat, though he gets points if he does. You may or may not suck his cock, but you'll get bonus points if you do. And none of this will happen unprotected. And when he asks if you have anything, he'll be asking for a condom and when you ask if he has anything, you'll be asking if he has diseases and then your knees will be pressed against his chest and his cock will be inside you and god you're wet and it feels so good and someone should find better words for all this than *god god god* which is what you say because this is casual sex so you won't use his name and you make small moans because you're supposed to and he makes small grunts in response and the weird thing is, you're ridiculously turned on suddenly by the noises you're making and it's as though they're real rather than just performed and it must be that way for him too, since he reaches back and grabs your hair so your head is immobilized and he's fucking you hard and it's so hot suddenly and you slide your hand between your bodies to play with your clit and it's hard to even do that because you're so wet but it doesn't take much at this point, you come, gasping, your cunt tightening and spasming around him and he slaps into you hard again and again and now he's almost shouting as he pulls out of you, rips the condom off his cock and shoots all across your belly then flops down on your bed beside you, breathing fast, sweating. You wait just long enough not to be insulting, then cross the room to grab your towel and wipe your tummy off. You throw the towel to him and lie back down.

And you or he crack a joke and you banter and he asks if you sound like you do because of porn movies and you say no, you've always sounded like this and you worry that you sound wrong, but no one's ever said anything before and maybe he runs his hand over your hair or maybe you curl your arm around his and in the next ten minutes he will dress and go since it's a weeknight and you both have to work in the morning and you trade phone numbers and emails and you think about calling, you do, you want him to call but aren't crushed when he doesn't because it was really just sex and there are so many men around and it's not that you're hurt exactly but you don't understand if you both had a good time why he doesn't call you. You won't call him since you're just as tough as he is and there are three others just like him this week and you'd tell your close friends about all this but they wouldn't understand, they'd just worry about you, so you'll just keep it to yourself and whatever and who the hell cares, it was fun. You had a good time. You'd do it again on purpose and you will. You will, since some day, all too soon, you and all these men will be quite dead.

wild kingdom

Early on, she realized things wouldn't work out between them, but she liked this one and was fruitlessly trying to find some way they could ride into the sunset together. They were sitting on the couch, drinking petit syrah, and she asked *If you were an animal, which one would you be?* And her lover responded, *Gee, I don't know. What kind of animal would you be?* She didn't have to think about it. She was a bunny. A wild bunny. Her nose would twitch and at nightfall, she'd hop out of her warren and eat leafy green things and she'd live gently and fuck rampantly and raise a fine brood and be the favorite animal of young girls and have little defense except her quickness, but inevitably one day her speed would fail her, and a predator would catch her tired, worn down, and close its jaws around her throat—*Now,* she asked her lover, *how about you?*

You know, I've never really thought about it, to tell you the truth, her lover said, pouring more wine.

A week later, they went to the zoo. *What about a lion?* she asked, their ears full of large-cat snarls. *Not really my style,* said her lover. *Maybe a black bear?* she asked, watching one rip the bark off a tree with its powerful claws. *No, not so much,* came the reply. *I think I'm probably something like a chimp.* Her face furrowed. What would a chimp do with a rabbit? *Did you see that news story about the chimp in San Francisco that ripped the face right off a man?* she asked, brightening, her nose full of monkey musk. *No. Must have missed that one. Okay, maybe not a chimp.* Neither of them spoke for quite some time, far past the penguin enclosure.

She began to watch the cable animal shows regularly. The feeding habits of ducks. Snakes inhaling rodents. Lions ripping gazelles. Sharks and seals. Spiders and flies. Foxes and rabbits. She found herself aroused.

She took to wearing angora on their dates and pinning her hair up, baring the back of her neck. *What about a fox?* she asked. *What is with you and this animal thing, anyway*, her lover wanted to know. *Why is this so important to you?*

It wasn't going to work out. But she was going to give it everything she had. The back of her neck was naked and aching for the brutal clench of jaws, that terminal snap.

cherchez la femme

Where is she? Where is the next dead girl? Ohio? Poughkeepsie? Hollywood? Baghdad?

How do you find her? Where can she be? How do you know it's her out of hundreds of thousands of girls? Do you know she's the one from the first time you see the arc of her smile, or is it over time, over chance collisions and accidents of conversation that snap the world closed and leave just the two of you? Is she someone who you've known for years, suddenly made new in a striking new way, one comment that suddenly changes her, irretrievably, from a corpse into a dead girl, your lover? The toe tag becomes a toe ring, the sheet becomes a dress, the body becomes a girl, a girl becomes the girl, your girl, your very own girl, made of history and blood, staying in your arms for as long as you stay convenient or compelling or in love. There is nothing more than the linguistic change from "girl" to "girlfriend."

You think your true love isn't out there? She can't find you? Not true. Stay still. All the dead girls, they keep coming, stiff-legged and stagger-stepped and one of them has the walk, left, right, left, and yours, that walk that leads right into your heart. Here she is, covered in blood, screaming those words that might be your name. It's a birthcry for both of you, a new beginning, as she toddles towards you, freshly dead and ready for love, rushing, openmouthed, head first.

introducing linda lovelace as herself

Helen? Helen, I'm home. I hope I'm not interrupting anything.

I see you're still the most beautiful girl in the world.

I'm going to slide up and down the banister.

How come you never had any superstar ego problems, anyway?

He wants warm supper.

Is it true you're on the cover of *Esquire*, with a yummy five-page spread in *Playboy*?

No, maybe later.

Does all this get you off?

Oh, sure.

I see you're still the most beautiful girl in the world.

Yeah, I'm fine.

A lot of women's liberation types see you as exploited, just as a male fantasy dream girl. That being able to be balled in your throat makes you just the most esoteric love slave around …

What makes you say that? It's us, the way we live. All right, what are you doing with your life? With who?

They say the story is just one long male fantasy, you know,

the sexually insatiable girl who makes it her whole life to please men ...

There, that's it. I'll never forget "what's his name."

I always did sense a certain envious undercurrent, like when Blair Sabol wrote in the *Village Voice* about a group of feminists discussing you at some consciousness-raising group and she said, "Suddenly talking about 'Deep Throat' we realized the real problem: NO one is getting laid anymore."

Look, Helen, there's got to be more, that's just it. I can't get married.

Oh, you must realize the effect you have on people ... some of them.

It wouldn't matter, I'd be miserable and I'd make him miserable, too.

How do you get along with all these celebrities I hear you're cavorting around with?

Sex. Sex. I don't enjoy it. All right, that's not altogether right. It makes me feel sort of tingly all over and then ... nothing.

Has it all taken over your personal life?

I mean, there should be more to sex than a lot of little tingles. There should be bells ringing, dams bursting, bombs going off, something.

It's beautiful to see you sitting here in jeans; if anything, you're more relaxed and open than the last time I talked to you. How come you never had any superstar ego problems, anyway?

Helen, please be serious. No. Never.

Have you taken any acting lessons or, say, comedienne lessons?

What do you mean? I'm not doing it right? I mean, how many ways are there? How?

Do you really have any idea how the very-physical Linda Lovelace has shaken up a hell of a lot of females in this country?

Okay, the way I feel, I'll try anything. Well, what now?

How about those lowdown articles in the sex newspapers and some of those weirdo photos?

Fourteen, last I count [unintelligible]. Look, this was your idea. What are we gonna do?

Listen, a bit of ancient history. Didn't you once tell me you used to consider giving head unclean and taboo, unnatural, even?

Sure I did and it was great, but so what? Not really like bells ringing and dams bursting and bombs going off.

Do you have any kind words for the legion of ladies out there, Lovelace fans all? Just a few teeny hints about getting it on?

Please be serious. What can I do?

You've got to get your head together, then, in more ways than one.

A doctor? I don't understand. A mental block?

I can well imagine lots of people gagging their brains out around the country.

No, I don't think so. You're getting me all wet. Please stop it.

You've got to get your head together, then, in more ways than one.

Listen, Doctor, please. I'm not turned off to sex. I enjoy it. In fact, I could spend the rest of my life getting laid. I don't know. Something's missing. Yes—there should be more to it than a lot of little tingles. I want to hear bells. Bombs. And dams bursting. Bombs bursting in air.

Impossible.

Please be serious. Yes. I want to hear bells. And bombs.

Impossible.

No, I don't think so. If you tell me somebody forgot his watch, I'll . . .

It goes very deep.

A cock? Of course I don't have one. I'm a woman.

Impossible.

Are you sure? Well, I'll be damned.

I think that's what made the film a success, the fact that you were so obviously having a ball, obviously getting off.

That's not funny.

Could you always give such great, complete head, or did you have to learn?

Giving head?

I think that's what made the film a success, the fact that you were so obviously having a ball, obviously getting off.

Sort of excited. You'll laugh. I get excited in here. Ahhh ahhh ahhh ahhh. What?

Did your experiences being forced into prostitution and pornography turn you off to sex?

[sobbing] That's easy for you to say. Suppose your balls were in your ear. Like what? Deep what?

Could you always give such great, complete head, or did you have to learn?

No, I try but I choke. You make it sound so easy.

What's your relationship with the feminist movement now?

Well, what have I got to lose?

Has anyone been too large for you?

Oh, Doctor Young, how can I ever repay you? You've saved my life, I'm a fulfilled woman! I've heard the bells at last! Oh, Doctor Young, marry me! I want to be your slave!

You are, Linda Lovelace, in addition to being probably one of the most beautiful creatures I've ever seen, the newest sex superstar in New York. No, more than that, you've become a kind of cult heroine.

What do you mean? You can't marry me? Oh, no. Oh, you're not getting off that easy. You've shown me the way and now you want to throw me out on the street, to go from one man to another?

Have you ever made a film before, or what's your experience up to *Deep Throat*?

> *What are you, crazy?*

And you're not in favor of censorship?

> *It's all your fault, don't you understand? I need it, I need love. I don't understand.*

What should the government do about pornography?

> *I don't know anything about physiotherapy.*

Do you have any sexual fantasies you'd like to see done on the screen, maybe somebody special you'd like to go down on or something?

> *Would you really, Doctor Young? Oh, Doctor Young, when can we start? The sooner the better. Will I need anything?*

Your billing in *Deep Throat* says, "Introducing Linda Lovelace as Herself."

> *Tell me, Mr. Moore, how do you feel now?*

You don't act or speak the way I expected from your movie and your book.

> *I'm so glad.*

Does your openness about your own sexuality threaten many of the men you meet?

> *You don't know how good that makes me feel, to know that I've been of some help to you.*

What's your attitude towards marriage?

> *I'll be glad to, Mr. Moore, but are you sure you can afford it?*
> *These are expensive treatments, you know.*

What should the government do about pornography?

> *Ohhh, I need a big, strong man.*

As you lived her, what's the character of Linda Lovelace?

> *Who are you? And what do you want? Please, don't hurt me.*
> *You can have anything you want, but please don't hurt me.*
> *Don't hurt me.*

Did your experiences being forced into prostitution and pornography turn you off to sex?

> *Please, don't hurt me.*

Why do you think that is?

> *I'm sorry, Wilbur, let's do it again. I'll do better this time.*

Did your experiences being forced into prostitution and pornography turn you off to sex?

> *You're so masterful, Wilbur. I can't help myself.*

As you lived her, what's the character of Linda Lovelace?

> *You're so masterful, Wilbur. I just can't help myself I get all*
> *weak when you come in with that mask.*

Your billing in *Deep Throat* says, "Introducing Linda Lovelace as Herself." Did people believe you were literally that character?

Let's go to bed, Wilbur. You've got me all hot.

If the censors permit it.

Okay, Masked Marvel. Anything you say. You know I'd do anything for you.

So what are you doing now?

No, I mean it, really. You've got me all tingly inside.

They say the story is just one long male fantasy, you know, the sexually insatiable girl who makes it her whole life to please men …

Oh, Wilbur, I like you but I can't marry you.

It goes very deep.

It's not just that. I believe you. It's just, well, the man I marry has to … the man I marry has to have a nine inch cock. Wilbur, it's my fault, not yours.

I see you're still the most beautiful girl in the world.

It's all Doctor Young's fault.

Oh, you must realize the effect you have on people … some of it?

Wilbur, why don't you give him a call. Maybe he could do something. You know, like an operation or some silicone injections?

Your billing in Deep Throat says, "Introducing Linda Lovelace as Herself." Did people believe you were literally that character?

Maybe, it's worth a try.

Tell me about that "new journalist" who did one interview with you and followed you all the way to Miami. He kept saying he had to have "carnal knowledge" of you.

Come on, let's give him a call. Oh, Wilbur!

re dress

It's a small dress, one she wore years ago. I slip it over my arm. That's the size of the whole dress: My hand sticks up inside a garland of lace where the head should be. My elbow pokes out instead of her feet. My arm instead of a baby, a girl. I match my fingertips to the thumb and I've made a duck's head. I make my little girl speak. *Quack*, she says. *Quack quack.* My duck daughter could catch a softball, could hold it, could throw away. She will never leave me.

*

It's a small dress, my first real cocktail dress, but I still fit into it. I slip it over my head when Bob and the kids are out. I pin up my hair, play Sinatra. I never liked Sinatra. I'm supposed to like Sinatra. I pin my hair up, my head proud above the satin ruffle. My elbow is cocked at a perfect angle to my ribcage as I go to the party in the bedroom. I chat in the mirror and laugh and laugh. *I work in a bank*, I say. *I'm not that kind of girl*, I say. *Cosmopolitan*, I say. The cat admires my sway. I've still got it. The front door opens and I scramble to shove every one in the closet, tell them *shush*. I still feel the satin on my skin. It will never leave me.

*

It's a small dress, one I wore when I was little. Now I couldn't fit my leg into it. A doll would barely fit into it. I find it in a drawer one day when I am getting rid of those things I never wear and don't remember acquiring. I stick it over a hat on my dresser. It looks like a little lace Christmas tree. I stick a small jewelry box at the hem. Then another. I pull a sock out of my sock drawer and catch the mouth so that it hangs down. I pull a couple of earrings out and stick them through the dress for decoration. I hum Christmas carols until bedtime. That night, I dream of acres and acres of small girls and men with large axes.

*

It's a small dress, one I wore when I was little. I'm bigger now, too big for this dress. I slip it over his head. It's the size of his whole body: His head sticks up inside a clown ruffle of lace. His sneakers peek out from under the hem. *It's a little long on you, too long.* He'll trip on it, he'll ruin it. *No I won't,* he says. Outside the dress, he throws softballs. Now I sit with him and put his makeup on. He puckers. *Now, do this,* I say. I show him how to make a popping sound with his lips together. *Pop,* he goes. *Pretty girl. My little girl. I will show you how to drink tea now with your pinky out.* His lip trembles and his eyes shine bright. This is his favorite game.

*

That night I dream of acres and acres of small girls with axes.

*

It's a small dress, but it's going to fit, it's going to fit, it's my sister's old dress but it's mine now. I can't seem to get it on right. My hand sticks up through what I think is the arm but it's the neck; the crisscross in back lifts and separates my breasts. I peel it over me and start over. *Come on,* I tell the dress. *This isn't a fight.* I shimmy into it and it cinches around my waist like a frightened child and won't go up or down. *Come on,* I tell the dress. *Mama!* cries the dress, its gabardine arms around me. *Mama!* I stand naked with the tire of a dress grasping me tight. *It's okay,* I say. *It's okay. Mama's right here.*

*

It's a small dress, one I would never fit into. But he's a small man, so it fits him perfectly. I slip it over his head. *What am I supposed to do?* I ask him. *Tell me I'm pretty,* he says. He's not pretty. He's ridiculous. His cock strains against the dress. It's disgusting. *Tell me I'm pretty,* he says. *Aren't you—*I start. I want to laugh. His neck is too thin but I've never noticed it before. What I want to say is *Aren't you fancy?* I can't look him in the eye. He can't look me in the eye. *Maybe this isn't—*he says, his eyes filling with tears. *I'm sorry,* he says. *No, no, I can. Really.*

*

Aren't you. Aren't you. Aren't you — pretty —

*

It's a small dress, one that would fit a girl much younger than she is. I thought she was four or five but it turns out she's six or seven right now. It looks like she is hiding a cat in tights. Something moves, solid and slow as anger. *Aren't you pretty,* I say. *What are you wearing under it? Will you show me?* Later, I will try to tell someone about her tights pussy.

*

Come on, I say. *This isn't a fight.* I stand naked. I chat in the mirror and laugh and laugh. *What are you wearing under it? Will you show me?* My cock strains against his dress. He's not pretty. *Mama!* He cries. I match my fingertips to the thumb and I've made a duck's head. It's going to fit. It's going to fit. His lip trembles and his eyes shine bright. This is our favorite game.

american gothic

No license plate, no make, no model, no witnesses. The hit-and-run love left me bleeding in the street, barely conscious, ripped apart. I'm soaring somewhere far above, watching, gone. There are people standing by my feet. I know this because I hear them say, "should've known …," "her fault …" and "seen it coming." I don't recognize the tops of any of their heads.

Women arrive with a cool white stretcher and dredge my body out of its deep pool, pull me back into the crash and burn of my flesh and we are moving. There are people by my sides saying "hopeless," "hold this," and "don't know if." I burrow down into the thick red muscle of my heart and I stay there until they force me back up, screaming and struggling and then nothing.

A small prick wakes me up. Then slowly, meticulously, a new border punctures its way up the length of my leg. I want to resist but can't move as my body is popped with more holes. I'm being stitched together, bit by bit.

Lovewrecked, could it be more love that puts you back together? What kind of love heals? Whose hands make everything better? My mother sewed. My body, my God, my mother, my country. It must be Betsy Ross, surgical mask in place, in her deep blue scrubs, tending to me, tender; she heroes me closed. She sews dreams into me, onto me. I almost seem to be myself but it's all her work. She never says a word as she enters me, over and over, pushes in, pulls out. Betsy.

When I wake up, everything's gone white. I ache with the miss of her all over. I thought I knew love, thought that love was shattered glass and sirens but really it's sutures and saline drips: It's the slow knit of bones coming back together and it's the throb in-between.

And Betsy is standing by my bedside. Betsy is pulling down her mask so that we can see each other for the first time, so we can kiss.

Her mouth tells me her name, tells me "grafts," tells me "success." She's not Betsy Ross at all. Her name is Mary Shelley. I am patched together with pieces of all the dead girls I've ever loved, have always loved. We're knitting together, they're scarring into me, and now we can never get away from each other. "I did it because I love you," says Mary. The dead girls and I look at her. We are, and love is, far, far more monstrous than I ever believed possible.

love poem after aretha franklin

you make me feel
you make me feel
you make me feel like a natural
　　　　　　　　disaster

the real deal

She doesn't want your little slave games, your come here, sit, roll over, play dead games. She doesn't need your dress-up games, your *yessir* games, your naughty spanky games. Her heart belongs to Daddy, she says, that's the real deal.

The men don't know but the little girls understand.

Daddy looks different from time to time. The first is Italian, short, with long hair slicked back in a ponytail. He is gentle and smiles at her a lot and plays Go Fish with her before they go to hotel rooms with strippers, and she watches as Daddy tells her, as Daddy shows her how it is done, how to hold the pipe while he sucks up, while her head starts to spin, her hands start to shake, she holds it for him with both hands while the stripper sucks his cock and Daddy says *YOU* think you got it? and she nods in time with her grinding teeth and Daddy takes her to the back room of an adult bookstore and the tokens are guttering down the slot, it reminds her of the pony rides outside of supermarkets as she bucks up and down against his hand, her legs spread apart with Daddy's hand between them, he's fucking her with his hand as they watch what she must learn to do, what big girls do. There are eye-level holes in the wall. In some of the holes, there are eyes, watching her. Daddy says *Stay here, I'll be right back. Don't move.* He sticks an electrode on each of her thighs. They prickle like the thistles she steps on in summer when she's not careful. He leaves the door unlocked. *Come back, Daddy*, she prays, over and over. *Don't let anyone else come in. I'm scared of the dark.* Daddy comes back. Her head is spinning. *Daddy?* she says. *Daddy's right here*, he says, and Daddy kept her safe, Daddy kept her safe. She throws her arms around him and he says, *Look what Daddy's got for you.* The pipe's in her mouth again, his hard cock's against her thigh and *Come on baby, doncha want it? Gonna do it for me? Be a good girl, come on, now. Do it for your Daddy.* She sucks and sucks and it gives her something to hang on to, holding something in her mouth. She sits on her hands. She is sitting on her coat. She's flying so fast. When she gets up, she's made the inside of her coat sticky.

They leave the booth and Daddy goes to look at movies to rent. A man comes up to her and gives her more tokens. She is a good little girl. She is the best little girl in the world. She'd do anything for her Daddy. So you can have the slave stuff, she doesn't need the play acting, the leather paddles, the collars, the whips. The next day, when she's a woman in her thirties, when she can't stop twitching and spinning, she will still know it's Daddy, she did it for Daddy, she's got tokens in her hand from a guy who watched her get fucked in a booth in the Tenderloin and she did that for Daddy she's a little girl she's not a whore and she's not ashamed she's *not* ashamed and she'd never have done it on her own but why bother asking when she doesn't regret it, not the sex though now she can't breathe, she can't breathe okay she's breathing now she can't stop shaking, her head is squeezing itself tight inside, and she takes valium and advil. Daddy—Daddy—she can't think, she rolls over, tries to sleep, her whole body aching, twitching, sore. Daddy is not her grinding teeth, Daddy is not here. She dreams of dancing baby aspirin. When she wakes up, she staggers to the bathroom. Don't talk to me about slave shit when you don't know shit about submission, she thinks. There's a difference between sex and submission. She stretches her upper body over the open toilet, waiting for the upthroat push out. I know all about doing anything I have to, she thinks. I know all about that slave shit. That's not sex.

But sex—Daddy's good to her. Daddy takes care of his baby.

Or the last one did. This Daddy, the new one, the one she just met, is not nice. He pulls the pipe away from her too soon, says, *That's enough for a little girl*, does not give it back. He makes her eat bologna sandwiches, four of them, one after the other until her stomach's about to burst and doesn't care that she doesn't eat meat and doesn't cut the crusts off. She is not sure Daddy is Daddy anymore. He sounds like Daddy with his *Come on baby, doncha want it? Gonna do it for me? Be a good girl, come on. Do it for your Daddy*, and when he is in the bathroom, she sneaks a hit off his pipe. They leave for a party where he tells her she's going to show the neighborhood fathers what a good girl she is. She says, *You said I was yours.* He says, *Do it for Daddy.* She runs outside crying and he grabs her, shoves her against the wall, lifts up her dress and spanks her. Her face is as red as her ass. Her face is wet, she's wet in between her legs. He shakes a bump out from a vial onto the triangle of hand between his first finger and thumb. He takes her back inside. She is ready to be a good little girl, the best girl, she wants to be Daddy's best girl.

She doesn't make it to work for two days. Her jaw is sore. She can't sit down because her ass is welted and her cunt is raw and Daddy leaves a message on her phone. It's Father's Day. She didn't call him. *Doesn't she love her Daddy?*

Then come the Daddies, a quick parade of Daddies, one and then another and then another. She is being fostered and shuttled off the one with large breasts and the knife who makes her shit on the floor like a baby and then punishes her for it and when she leaves, Daddy yells after her, *Family is family—I will always be here;* there's the Daddy who is her drug connection and he's ten years younger than she is and a head shorter and she's trying to kick now, doesn't want it, doesn't want any more mornings with a screwcap head and a horserace pulse, the stutter heart, except when she'll take it for what comes first and that's when she calls him because family will always be there but he just wants to watch tv and drink beer and she wants to—she doesn't know, but something, something—she doesn't want that *yessir* shit, that naughty spanky-spanky, keep-your-bottom-high shit, she wants the real shit, her heart belongs to Daddy and Daddy loves her Daddy loves her she knows Daddy loves her, like the Daddy she meets at the nightclub after someone dopes her drink and Daddy fucks her in his car, Daddy's blonde wig tipping on his head, the strap of his lingerie sliding over the side of his shoulder. *Daddy! likes! to! be! as! pretty! as! his! girl!* he puffs, as he stabs her with his cock. After, he cracks the car window and smokes a cigarette. *What's your name?* she asks him. *Daddy's enough for you to know*, he says. When she gets home, it's eight in the morning. She can't stop shaking. The sun is burning her. The world is ending, she thinks. She can't stand it. She takes two valium, sorry they're not twenty, sorry they're not fifty, sorry they'd never be enough and she's too tired to sob. No more, she thinks. No more. The apocalypse swarms up at her in a bright burst of black. Enough about that slave shit.

Doesn't Daddy always take care of her? The apocalypse swarms up.

It's a few months before she sees Daddy again, before she's ready to see Daddy again, before her high bottom is smacked into that room and she's a good girl, she reads her book like they tell her, she admits she is powerless, hasn't she always been powerless? and she is a star student, Daddy's prize pupil and now, Daddy lies on top of her, Daddy, hairless like a high school boy and talking in a low, calm voice. She loves how it feels when she takes Daddy's huge cock, when he lets her have it, when she's Daddy's special girl, Daddy's dime-tight nipples rubbing against hers and she doesn't need anything else right now and don't talk to her about that degradation shit, she's had enough of that *roll over, play dead* shit, all she needs is Daddy and Daddy's right here. She would've done all that shit without the pipe and they want her to be ashamed but she's not ashamed but she's crying, she doesn't know why, except

she thought she'd never be here again. Her heart belongs to
Daddy and Daddy loves her, and Daddy's going to take care of
her, *That's right, baby, ssssh, my baby*, Daddy says, lying on top
of her. It is too soon to tell, but she hopes Daddy, this Daddy,
will put electrodes on her thighs, will welt her ass, will want
her the way she wants Daddy, wants—Daddy's got his hand
up against her throat and her pulse is beating, beating. She is
safe and warm and when Daddy tightens his hand she can't
breathe she can't breathe. If she could move right now, she
would burrow her head into Daddy's warm, downy armpit, go
somewhere safer, but nothing that excites her has ever been
safe and her body is tied over and apart and against and away
and Daddy coos into her ear as Daddy's switchblade snaps to
attention, *You gonna do it for Daddy? You Daddy's good girl?*
She nods. *Look what Daddy's got for you*, he says, as he rubs
the handle of his knife against her cunt, the tip of the blade
just nipping the inside of her thigh and she is smiling. Wide.
Good girl, Daddy says, because she's a girl, she's no one's slave.
She doesn't want that *sit, stay, come* shit, none of that *roll over,
play dead* shit. She's home. She's home with Daddy, and that's
the real deal.

someone should write me a love poem
but i'm stuck doing it myself

1. when i was in high school, i had to memorize the conjugation of the latin verb "to love."

2. i have no idea what happened to my mother's wedding ring. last night at 12:17 AM, i really needed to know.

3. "beautiful" and "amazing" just mean "beautiful" and "amazing." nothing more.

4. i memorized the latin verb by singing the forms to the tune of "the mexican hat dance":

   amo
   amas
   amat

   amamus
   amatis
   amant

5. someone called at 1:19 in the morning. the area code is from somewhere in arizona. i don't think i know anyone in arizona. there wasn't a message.

6. if someone lets you sleep over and has to go to work while you're still asleep and they let you sleep in even though they don't really know you, it's nice to leave a thank you note. or make their bed.

7. i haven't been beautiful in days and i need more sleep. don't think about it too much. it doesn't mean a thing.

8. i have had my shirts altered so i can wear my heart on my
   sleeve.

9. told me i'm beautiful and amazing and where are you,
   who told me i'm beautiful and amazing, next time please
   write it down, i will be beautiful all day after i make the
   bed, amazing after i throw the latex away; how is it, the
   everywhere of our hands and no trace of handwriting
   anywhere

10. i still sing:

   amo
   amas
   amat

   amamus
   amatis
   amant

sentenced

it has been done and done and done to death   sick of the
suicides, sure   and nature's been done   to death
     is there really anything more to be said about geese? ever?
                    and please please no more poems about poems
the only thing worse   than poems   about poems
are poems about   love   I have committed my share
I have done my time   love always loses   inevitably
poems   outlive   the love
so maybe the answer is to stick   with the poems
                    but not poems about suicide
or geese   or poems   and especially not
about love   I admit I have a record   in the past
there was a time   when I committed love poems   but no more
I have paid   my debt to society and come back
rehabilitated   no more love   poems, you came
                         too late   lover   I'm sorry
          you took so long   to come but you're here
just in time for   global warming   poems or
meek shall inherit   poems
postmodern conundrum birdcage effervesce   poems
                    reader reception   poems
                    but no more   love poems   there are no
more   the first time you looked at me   poems
                    never a walking down
                    not a do not pass   go   do not collect
my lover's eyes   or even all my lovers' eyes
do not compare thee to a   mission street walk
smarting a shove shoulder into yours   not a single
motown you to morning, not a   singing in the shower
sweet morning sting of peppermint soap over our bodies
never that   first moment you looked at me
peeked back over your shoulder   leaning over your
motorcycle   that look   smirk that

smile   wanted to fuck   that smile right   off your face
put it back   never   a poem never   white briefs
not a   tumble   damp   poem of
no use crying   over   damp   tumble   dry
bright   white sheets no use crying over spilled ink
now look what you've gone and done   it's committed
to print   I guess you'll have to stay

glass onion

Sharon's so pregnant, there's no trace of the knife in her anymore. She's all curves. She's a gall on a goldenrod stem; round, firm. She's a twig with a plum hanging from the center, overfull, obscene, almost ready to burst because she's so ripe. The hushed violence of the natural world buzzes inches from her body.

She's flushed with the cram of two lives under her skin, and everything around her seems drenched with it. The air is thick and slow and the sun is the sweet ooze of melted butter. Heavy. She's humming "Love Me Do" and it comes out as a slow summer lullaby. Or a dirge.

She's nestled in my arms and the thick of her is as shocking as her weightlessness—she's a soap bubble as her hand drifts to my face, strokes the edge of it with her nails painted the color of blood. They're smooth and cool.

I want to put a record on, she says, and she floats over to the stereo, the baby leading the way.

She glides back over to the couch and I hold her carefully in my arms, afraid she'll rupture. She sighs and warm syrup comes out.

Obladi Oblada Life goes on, Oh!

The record sounds so far away, like it's coming from underwater. She swivels her face to mine, a Botticelli under sepia aspic.

This, she says. *This is good.*

I know. I know.

Just like this. Just like this forever.

Yes, I say. I say yes. And so it is. We stay on the couch, fade together like a silver gelatin print left in the sun.

La la la la

two women

Being with her is like watching a clock: The hands don't move and then suddenly, they're somewhere entirely different but absolutely familiar. She takes pride in her daily reincarnations, paints them in exacting detail.

This morning, she had vines growing out of her body. They trailed her steps, swept the floor behind her. By noon, she was rooted to the chair she ate breakfast in. I brought her water and her paints. And I left her to her doings. *Esto es quien soy,* she said. *¿Puedes amarme como esto?* I don't speak a word of Spanish, but somehow, I always know what she's saying. I tell her I love her any—every—way she comes. It's true. I do. But some incarnations are easier than others to deal with.

She crawls in bed beside me, presses her chest, her belly, her legs against the back of me. Our bed is a bus that crashes every night. Every sleep is surgery. I bring band-aids and clean sheets.

Today she awoke with the portrait of a man between her thick black eyebrows. "Who is that?" I ask her. "Do you love him?" *Mis pinturas,* she says, so I bring her the paints and a blank canvas. *Mi muerte,* she says, and I say, "No. Not yet."

My friends think I'm making my life more difficult, being in love with someone who is so radically different day to day. *You should leave,* they say. *You're getting thin. You're not sleeping.* They don't understand. Most days, I'm grateful. I see all of her and I'm always surprised. *She's in love with a man,* they say. I know. But she has enough love for me, too. *She'll leave you,* they say. "Probably," I agree. I tell them I'll always have my photographs of her. I take photographs of her in each incarnation. In the photographs, though, she always looks the same: braids wrapped to the top of her head, bright dress. No deer. No blood. No her. My lens misses most of her.

When we wake up tomorrow, there will be a monkey in our bed. I don't have to ask how it got there. It's not important. Two days from now, she will inhabit the body of a deer shot by hunters with at least seven arrows. More scars. More paints. She moans in her sleep. Her body hurts. I change the sheets in the morning and bring her fresh grass.

We both have rituals before sleep. Hers: She stares at a dark window at night. Not through, but at. The dark gifts her with a mirror. She watches herself stare back. She breathes a cloud onto the window. She traces a rectangle onto the glass, then a dot. The window is a door. With a knob.

My ritual before bed: I count her scars. *Como puedes tocarlas? Son tan feas.* "No," I say. "They're part of you." Pain is ugly, but survival isn't. She never paints her scars.

She's got cropped hair and a man's suit. She's holding her own hand, standing beside herself. She's a body on a gurney. She's giving birth. She's wearing bright red and blue and green and her hands are folded.

Lastima, she says, holding her scars in her arms. The clock says it's 2 AM. She stares at herself in the window, draws that door but this time, she reaches out her hand for the knob. It's going to spring open under her hand. *Vamos. Es hora.* I'd follow her anywhere.

organic

She didn't get much mail and even fewer packages, and she had always thought of herself as lucky in love until that day the liver showed up in the mail.

Who sent me this? she wondered. It came with a card signed *Your Secret Admirer.* There was no return address and it was postmarked locally. She tossed the dying hydrangea bouquet in the trash and put the vase in the sink. She settled the organ into the middle of her kitchen table, where the sun glittered on the meat.

She wasn't sure what to make of the liver hovering in its jar, lavender on the outside with a deep maroon underneath. She'd received chocolates before. She'd gotten flowers. She hoped someday, someone would give her their heart. But now, here it was, a liver.

Maybe, she thought, she's a girl only good enough for lesser organs—the non-poetic ones and organs you needed but could deal with only having one of: lungs or kidneys. She supposed there was a third tier of organs you didn't need that you could send away easily: appendices, spleens. *Better second-tier*, she thought, *than third.*

She realized that she didn't even know whether this liver was male or female, if livers had genders on their own, or how she knew this was a human liver in the first place. If this liver was female, did it make her a lesbian? She didn't know. She just didn't know.

The liver floated in its jar. If it had eyes, it would have stared at her wistfully. *Face facts*, she told herself. *Right now, that liver is all alone in the world and so are you.* She began to think perhaps she was lucky in love after all: Chocolates get eaten. Roses die. Hearts fail all the time. This pickled liver was hers forever. Maybe this was the real deal, the true blue.

There was a bottle of crème de menthe in the cabinet under the sink left over from last year's bridal shower for her sister. She pulled it out of the cupboard and poured a sticky, pine-colored tablespoon into a teacup and sat back down. *Here's to you*, she said, raising her glass to the liver, fetal in its jar, *and here's to me. Down the teeth and over the gums* ... the thickened mouthwash slapped her teeth. *Here's to us*, she thought, then aloud: *Here's to us.*

calliope

I've got a thing going on with a magician's ex-assistant. Things ended badly between them. After the rabbit died, he pulled a disappearing act, leaving her sawed in half in the black box. She's trying so hard to pull it together, but really, she's a fraction of the woman she once was. Two halves, to be exact.

Which is not without its benefits: Sex with two people has never seemed more like a threesome; it's even worth the bloodstains on the sheets left by either half of her waist, but it's hard to watch her getting dressed afterwards, dragging her top half towards the bottom, sliding herself almost whole. Sometimes after sex, her top slips off walking to the bathroom. Her legs blindly stumble on, tripping heels over head on her way back to bed. She gets back in between the sheets; arms, then back; ass, then heels; she aligns herself and meekly says, *TaDaaa.*

People will tell you that love only breaks your heart, but it really can break you all over: in half, in quarters, eighths, sixteenths. I tell her she's lucky he didn't leave her after the box-of-swords trick—the one where she's in the black box but he sticks sword after sword into diagonal after diagonal across her tender body—or the metal blades trick, where he chopped her into mincemeat. *It could have been so much worse,* I tell her, *but you are such a strong woman,* and she nods through her sobs, staggers towards the bathroom. I'm not sure she knows it's true. I think all she knows is that it feels like hell right now, that it's hard to heal when you fall apart, bloodily, time after time, hour after hour, day after day. *Strength,* she says, *is its own kind of curse. It's so hard to keep myself here,* she says, balancing her upper body carefully on her lower. As she bends for a Kleenex in the dark, I am thinking of other girls: the girl I loved who fell in love with a lion—she lost her head over it—we just necked a lot; of the girl who fell in love with the tightrope, got addicted to getting high wired and nothing else was enough; all the beautiful, damaged women who have come through my life and I wonder what would have happened if I'd met them sooner, what they were like before they were so badly wounded. All this time I thought I'd been kissing, but maybe I'm always doing mouth-to-mouth resuscitation, kissing dead girls in the hopes that the heart will start again. Where there's breath, I've heard, there's hope.

I hear a soft slip and thud in the bathroom, a small, damp dragging as she recomposes herself. I hear her, through sobs, choke out, *TaDaa*, and see the swell of her curves, upper, then lower, as she slowly, carefully, balances on her feet and walks gently back, doing the proudest, slowest strut through the darkened room. She's lit by the confetti of carnival lights coming though the window from somewhere very far away.

living legend

"Dream as if you'll live forever. Live as if you'll die tomorrow."
—James Dean

being james dean
isn't easy.
even james dean
couldn't do it for long

so now it's up to me
to be the kind of boy
girls want to fuck
boys want to be

boys want to fuck
girls want to be
in order
to be
james dean

in order
to fuck
james dean
in the leather bar

bathroom, putting cigarettes out
on his arm
ashes to ashes, dust to dust,

that kind of
prove-me-
right-here rough
come on

with fingers too fast
for *please*, knees
smacked on the tile
nose full of piss

and clorox, handful
of your hair,
see, that's
the kind

of james dean i am.
i see the way you look at me
when your cock is in me
james dean

the way you cry out
when my knuckles find you
slick inside.
one step past tender

is where you find raw
and that's where
we're driving
tonight

where i find you
in me,
james dean
when we

fuck on the barstool james dean
against a chainlink fence
rebel without a
daddy's on his belly for you james dean

momma's on her back
and now i'm taking baby
for the ride
of her life

straight from my james dean hips
with curves as sharp
and dangerous
as a rebel boy's death

watch us as we go
as we are one
two
one

red hot tail light flares
as we scramble
as we soar

as we push right over
as we one into one
james dean
as we one

into one
faster
than the speed
of death

coney island baby
"Man, I swear, I'd give it all up for you." —*Lou Reed*

I'm falling I've fallen I'm found for someone who's nothing like anyone I've ever met before. I'm falling for someone and it has all the earmarks: the queasy tummy, the sudden shudders, the agnostic body that listens to nothing but its own indivine will. This is no dead story. This is a live wire, fresh bait, a deafening smash and roar of arrival, your hand in mine. You are someone I've known for years. You are someone I've just met—always, somehow, just met. My lover, my sweetheart, my breath-mint fresh stun gun, this is an I've never done this and I want to do this; this is an I'm tired, just let me rest; this is an I'm gun shy, I've got so many wounds there's no place to put more scar tissue and I'm done; this is an I can't, not again; this is a call to action; this is an I'm scared by everything I've learned; this is how did you, how did I; this is a why bother even trying since everybody tells me they know how this ends, but it comes down like faith, like a roller coaster and there are parts where it feels like you're going to die and even at the good parts you think you're going to heave but there's nothing like it, nothing nothing like it, when you stretch your arms into the sky and you scream, and your mouth wide open, looking, wide-eyed at the one who is suddenly, frighteningly, right beside you and maybe, maybe if you're lucky, the ride is good and maybe, maybe you end up, for a little while, seeing something better—doing something better—being someone better than how you started off, climbing slowly up, slowly up slow slowly up and maybe just maybe this time we can perilous   stay

maps and legends

Does it hurt? Of course it hurts.

Knowing I am going away past the sharp edge of the world, she knows we need magic, we need magic stronger than words since just words cannot save us. I follow her to the place where the machines hum and draw blood since we need strong magic, need to rip the skin, let blood, and change the body for life, so it knows.

This is where the journey begins. We follow royalty here, we follow gangs here, we follow brides-to-be here, we follow prisoners here, we follow thieves and sailors here. We walk through the open door and look for what we need.

This is where the journey begins. I leave now, or I will not be gone for months, or I will never leave. Does it hurt? Of course it hurts. Home is where the heart is or home is where the body is. I travel light. I never let go of her hand, home. She is my heart.

We walk through the open door and look for what we need. Beyond the edge of the world, there are dragons. Their pictures are on the wall, like WANTED posters. WANTED: what we need. I am already more woman than girl, so there is no need to slit open my chin, mark the equator. No need for love charms, no pierced hearts, no roses. No stars, one for each year behind bars, no barbed wire for an imprisoned life. Not the pig and the rooster to keep me from drowning, nor the legend H-O-L-D / F-A-S-T—there will be no ropes where I go.

Serious magic: When you bride the machine, you can never go back, even after death: This is where the body was found, before the edge, before the dragons. This is how they know the body: White female, 5'11", 160 pounds. Identifying marks: Even after days in the water, death knows you by your magic: the water swelling the body, the body more water than blood or bone, and still the body speaks after death, says: Blood, North, South, Sailor, Thief, King, Queen, Ace. The Spade brings luck, as does the dice. But we need more than luck. Protection is more than luck. There are dragons past the edge. I never let go of her hand.

Birds know magic like they know home. Their hearts beat too fast for land and carry them into the air, beat, beat, a signal on a drum or a trumpet, a knocking or strong pulsation, beat, my heart, her, beat a tattoo into my ribs. My heart is in my mouth. I swallow. Birds know magic like they know home, where the swallows return every year without fail, and begin rebuilding. The machine builds its bride, rips into the skin. You can never go back.

We tell the man: Swallows, we need swallows. He nods. He knows. He crosses me over the equator, the line between, over the edge, there are dragons out there. He nods and says, "Where?"

Place is everything. Either you are home or you are not. Either you are on one side of the equator or the other. Either you are safe or. She speaks. "On her hands. Protect her hands, so that nothing falls through them." He nods. "On her heart. Protect her heart, so nothing can hurt there." He nods again, slowly, the machine purrs harder, waiting. "On her throat, so nothing can stop her voice when she needs it; on her legs, so nothing can keep her from running, on her head, so—"

—so she sings the song of the machine and the machine sings my blood and swallows, my hands, my heart, the swallows will bring me home when it is time to rebuild; place is everything, you can never go back. There are dragons out there.

We walk through the open door. Out on the edge, this is where the body was found, where the journey begins: I am sailor, thief, queen. I am home. I am only girl in the spaces between powerful magic, what swallows bring in their mouths to nest with. Their hearts beat too fast to keep them on the earth, does it hurt? Her heart beats a tattoo into my ribs, blood, of course it hurts, and every year, WANTED, the swallows return home. H-O-L-D / F-A-S-T: On this journey, I never let go of her hand.

Printed in the United States
by Baker & Taylor Publisher Services